Radically Inclusive Teaching With Newcomer and Emergent Plurilingual Students

Radically Inclusive Teaching With Newcomer and Emergent Plurilingual Students

Braving Up

**Alison G. Dover and
Fernando (Ferran) Rodríguez-Valls**

Foreword by Ofelia García

TEACHERS COLLEGE PRESS

TEACHERS COLLEGE | COLUMBIA UNIVERSITY
NEW YORK AND LONDON

Published by Teachers College Press,® 1234 Amsterdam Avenue, New York, NY 10027

Copyright © 2022 by Teachers College, Columbia University

Front cover design by Pete Donahue.

The research reported in this book was made possible (in part) by a grant from the Spencer Foundation (#10021888). The views expressed are those of the authors and do not necessarily reflect the views of the Spencer Foundation.

Library of Congress Cataloging-in-Publication Data is available at loc.gov

ISBN 978-0-8077-6640-2 (paper)
ISBN 978-0-8077-6641-5 (hardcover)
ISBN 978-0-8077-8075-3 (ebook)

Printed on acid-free paper
Manufactured in the United States of America

Contents

Additional readings and professional learning resources on the
companion website at tcpress.com/dover-resources

Foreword

The theme of "braving up" that is the subtitle of this book is one that resounds with my own work. In the book that I co-edited with Maite Sánchez on transformative translanguaging espacios, braving up is inherent in the subtitle "Sin Miedo!," or in English, "without fear." I now pause and wonder: Why do we need braving up and fearlessness to teach in ways that are inclusive, justice-oriented, and culturally and linguistically sustaining of emergent bilingual learners? Isn't that what all education should be?

The pedagogical practices that Dover and Rodriguez-Valls describe in this book are seen as "radical" and needing "bravery." And yet, as the authors describe, they are only ways of educating from linguistically, culturally, and community-anchored standpoints. Grounded in the work that the authors have done since 2015 in Southern California with teachers of 7- to 12-year-old newcomer emergent bilinguals in a project they call "Language Explorers," the book and the companion website offer important principles and examples of how teachers and students can co-construct meaningful learning experiences that are inclusive of *all* of them. This book foregrounds practice, and yet is rich in theory. In many ways, it contributes to three important theoretical/practical advances: (1) the reconceptualization of professional development and alternative educational spaces, (2) a continuum of teaching and learning, and (3) an inclusive understanding of language.

The processes described herein nourish the teachers' professional expertise and agency, starting by uncovering their own identities and experience. By taking personal and professional risks, teachers open new paths for themselves and for their students. One interesting idea in the book is that teachers must bring their whole selves into the classroom. Bravery is needed for teachers to experience activities, discourse, ideas, and emotions as co-learners. The gaze shifts from that of teachers as White education experts to the texts of minoritized communities as authoritative. In this reciprocal relationship, much is gained. Unlike other books that describe alternative educational spaces, the intent of the authors is to help educators reimagine what schooling can and should look like.

Teaching and learning are presented here not as separate processes, but as a continuum that engages the authors, teachers, and students as co-conspirators, co-learners, and co-planners of the experience. Based on the South African principle of Ubuntu that "I am because you are," the teachers are engaged in a different pattern of socialization, one that both disrupts the institutional rhetoric about emergent bilingual students and also engages them with their students' agency and strengths. The book title is instructive in this way, for the inclusion is not only of student diversity, but also of teachers. The teachers are not all bilingual, and not all are language teachers. The teachers and students in the book reflect all human variation. The most important aspect of this multidirectional teaching then becomes how to provide opportunities for equity in the co-learning process. This dynamism in the joint process of teaching/learning produces the ability to *pivot* to the specific situation, and so the book also provides examples of work produced online during the pandemic.

Finally, the conceptual grounding of the book is on an inclusive understanding of language. Although teachers and students are linguistically diverse, named languages are not the focus. The goal is not the development of "English," or of students' "first languages." These concepts, which are so prevalent in the literature on the education of emergent bilinguals, are absent from this book. Rather, emphasis is on students' and teachers' languaging, their doing of language in ways that are generative and that communicate who they are and what they can learn together. In so doing, teachers and students take up and extend the concept of translanguaging, going beyond named languages and beyond simply the acquisition of a "second language."

The paradigm that Dover and Rodriguez-Valls have co-developed with teachers and students focuses on arts-based multiliteracies, extending translanguaging to truly encompass the multimodalities that have been left out of much language education. It is through arts that teachers first experience the ideological and political shifts that allow them to imagine how to change the world and schools, and then to produce curricular and pedagogical shifts.

Perhaps of most value to teachers will be the activities or scaffolds that Dover and Rodriguez-Valls develop to ensure the engagement of teachers and students with complex and controversial ideas, and in order to develop individual and collective accountability. Carefully and gradually, we are presented with activities that move from visual representations to linguistic representations. Poetry, picture books, portraits, mapping, caminatas, comics, icebreakers, and narrative writing are used not only to provide the rich educational context that emergent bilinguals deserve, but also to brave up and clearly reveal the strength of diverse students that traditional schools have hidden for so long.

—Ofelia García
The Graduate Center, City University of New York

Acknowledgments

Courageous, intrepid, bold, daring, lionhearted, fearless, courageous, and *plucky* are some of the adjectives that describe all the participants, designers, and creators of this brave adventure of radically transforming how we learn and teach newcomer and emergent plurilingual students.

Thank you to all the courageous teachers and instructional assistants who gave up their summers and weekends to challenge themselves and their students to create new and visionary [trans]languaging spaces. Your intrepidness is an example for all the educators who are committed, like you, to "brave up" their pedagogies and methodologies.

Cảm ơn to all the Language Explorers/Students/Scholars for being bold in your work. Your creativity, knowledge, and wisdom are bigger than any language constraint or standardization. Using Freire's (2005) words, you are an example of students who dare to learn. You are the new generation of cultural and linguistic advocates. It brings us hope to know our future is in your hands.

谢谢!to all the lionhearted administrators in each school district where Language Explorers have created new paths. It is not easy to develop linguistic biomes in habitats ruled by exams, grades, and démodé measures of learning and achievement. Yet you were fearless in providing what you thought education should be: a transformational practice. Yes, you are the ones leading the landscape. We are especially appreciative for the vision and leadership of Renae Bryant, Laura Dale Pash, Diana Fujimoto, Vanessa Galey, Roxanna Hernandez, Michael Matsuda, and Cynthia Petitt, without whom the programs featured in this book could not have flourished.

Gracias to all our colleagues at the College of Education at California State University, Fullerton. You had the courage to support and trust our ideas and vision. Having you as champions of our languaging vision pushed us to dream bigger and broader. Once more, we reached higher, we taught taller, and we impacted larger.

감사합니다 to all our partners and sponsors for their pluckiness. When we explained our thoughts and wrote our proposals, they saw beyond the written and text and oral expressions. They felt us as two unapologetic educators who are here to radically change teaching and learning. And for that we are thankful.

Last, but not least, we want to thank our families, for nourishing, celebrating, challenging, and commiserating with us as we wrote. Corabella, Alia, and Tony: you bring me so much joy. Thank you for showing me each day how many reasons I have to stretch and grow. I love you. Thank you also to the many who parented, mentored, trudged the road beside, and believed in me as I learned to believe in myself. You taught me how to be brave, and I am so very grateful.

Gràcies a totes les persones que m'han inspirat durant aquesta aventura d'escriure. El caliu de la família a Catalunya i el recolzament i sentiment del Cal Tortugueta a Califòrnia son imprescindibles per poder fer de les idees i de les lletres quelcom radical. Sense tots vosaltres no hi ha valentia.

CHAPTER 1

Braving Up: The Journey Begins With Questions

It is hard to accept that 2 decades into the 21st century, schools continue to struggle to meet the academic needs of their students, and especially students who are not White[1], not English-dominant, not wealthy, not Christian, not normatively abled, not cisgender, or otherwise not privileged within U.S. educational systems. This is despite the tremendous research base regarding the importance and impact of multicultural and culturally responsive education; the introduction of teacher certification requirements related to teaching culturally and linguistically diverse learners; and the myriad state and federal programs intended to increase equity of access, experience, and outcome. The problem, clearly, is not that educators and policymakers are unaware of the problem, but rather that we have been remarkably ineffective in solving it.

In *Radically Inclusive Teaching with Newcomer and Emergent Plurilingual Students: Braving Up*, we examine the ideological, curricular, pedagogical, and political factors that shape the daily experiences of students who are new to the United States and in the process of incorporating English into their linguistic repertoires. Throughout, we challenge readers to consider how each of us—at times intentionally and at others unknowingly—participate in educational and linguistic practices that marginalize, minoritize, and silence the very students we purport to serve.

In the chapters to follow, you will meet teachers and educational leaders who are challenging themselves and their schools to do education differently, to brave up and re-vision classrooms as places where newcomer and emergent bilingual students' identities, languaging, and humanity are not only invited, but affirmed and amplified. You will also hear directly from newcomer students themselves, as they courageously explore their identities, experiment with their voices, and share their vision of what a radically inclusive community could be. We invite you to join us, not in simply implementing a new teaching strategy or program, but in critically reimagining what it means to teach and learn in plurilingual K–12 classrooms.

WHY THIS BOOK?

American schools are exceptionally diverse places, enrolling almost 51 million students and speakers of more than 400 languages (United States Department of Education, 2015, 2021). In California, 42% of public school students speak a language other than English at home (California Department of Education, 2021a), rendering it the most linguistically diverse state in the country. Nevertheless, monolingualism continues to be the norm within most educational settings, limiting opportunities for all students to leverage and expand their linguistic repertoires. This is not accidental; educational systems systematically privilege assimilation into the dominant culture at the expense of heterogeneity of identity, language, ability, and expression. While ideologies of normalcy (that is, binary constructs that define what is "normal" and what is "abnormal") impact all students, the implications are especially significant for students from minoritized and marginalized groups, including immigrants and newcomer students, whose very existence marks them as "different" or "abnormal" (Annamma, Boelé, Moore, & Klingner, 2013).

The impact of this ideology is profound; research attests to the degree that newcomer students, and especially those who do not speak the dominant language at their school site, struggle to feel academically, socially, and relationally connected at school and in their community (Fruja Amthor & Roxas, 2016; Rodríguez-Valls, 2016; Suárez-Orozco, Suárez-Orozco, & Todorova, 2008; Yeon Kim & Suárez-Orozco, 2015). In addition to linguistic exclusion, many newcomers are navigating significant social and economic pressures, including high levels of poverty, unwelcoming social or political climates, and experiences of racism and discrimination (Choi, 2013; Suárez-Orozco, Pimentel, & Martin, 2009). Moreover, newcomer students are far from culturally or linguistically monolithic, and even those students in schools with a large population of newcomers may not encounter teachers or students with whom they share a language, sociocultural identity, or lived experience (Fruja Amthor & Roxas, 2016).

There is a wide research base underscoring the academic and social benefits of culturally and linguistically responsive teaching (Aronson & Laughter, 2016; Dover, 2009; Lee, 2010; Sleeter, 2011). However, newcomer and emergent plurilingual students are too often exposed to programs that neither value their cultural and linguistic richness nor embrace their identities as assets for their learning (Gee, 2004). Many school districts struggle to design and implement programs that both affirm newcomer students' cultural fortes and also empower them to use their social and linguistic capital as springs to expand their social mobility (Fránquiz & Salinas, 2011; Freire & Valdez, 2017; Mitchell, 2012; Salinas, Sullivan, & Wacker, 2007). At the school site level, a complex constellation of institutional forces, including pressure toward standardization, monolingualism, monoglossia, and test-based accountability, can trouble teachers' efforts to center the immediate, localized, and situated needs of their students (e.g., Agarwal, Epstein, Oppenheim, Oyler, & Sonu, 2010; Fruja Amthor & Roxas, 2016; Picower, 2011; Sleeter, 2011). This results in the marginalization of culturally and linguistically responsive teaching in K–12 and teacher education programs alike, undermining new and experienced teachers' development of the autonomy, agency, and self-efficacy necessary to enact social justice–oriented change (see Dover, Henning, & Agarwal-Rangnath, 2016).

It doesn't have to be this way. In this book, we draw on our experience working with hundreds of educators, and thousands of newcomer students, as they collaboratively examine and deconstruct language, identity, and culture through an exploration of high interest poetry, music, art, and young adult literature. In the process, students and educators analyze their unique and shared linguistic and cultural identities, explore multiple perspectives and lived experiences, and stretch their collective vision of what education should be. In the pages that follow, we explore the theories that guide our work, sharing classroom vignettes, resources, and scaffolds to support educators and leaders in considering how they might implement and institutionalize affirming, literacy-rich programming in their own classrooms and school sites.

WHAT DOES IT MEAN TO BE BRAVE?

Conceptually, our work is grounded in theories and practices of culturally and linguistically sustaining pedagogy (Paris & Alim, 2017), emergent curriculum (Dover & Schultz, 2018; Freire, 1970/2000), and translanguaging (Flores & García, 2013; García & Seltzer, 2016; Wei, 2018), in which educators embrace the literacies and discursive practices of multiple languages, model linguistic fluidity and risk-taking, and function as linguistic co-learners alongside their students. In addition to engaging and affirming students, culturally sustaining and social justice–oriented practices have a positive impact on student achievement, participation, sense of belonging in educational environments, identity development, and attitudes about school, especially among racially and linguistically marginalized students (see Aronson & Laughter, 2016; Bajaj & Suresh, 2018; Dover, 2009; Gay, 2000; Ladson-Billings, 1995; Oyserman, Harrison, & Bybee, 2001; Sleeter, 2011).

However, radically inclusive teaching is not simply about implementing curricular and pedagogical shifts, but ideological and political ones.

Many educators are themselves the products of K–12 and teacher education systems that reinforce monolingualism; in the United States, for example, plurilingual learning is often corralled into an isolated subset of designated bilingual classrooms, leading to the seemingly inextricable conflation of the notions of "academic language" and English. In order to transform the systems that silence and oppress plurilingual students, we must look deeply at our own role in creating and perpetuating those systems, including the impact of our assumptions, socialization, and enactments of languaging. This requires bravery, as we become willing to question ourselves, our colleagues, and our beliefs about teaching and learning.

In the chapters to come, we explore how diverse educators—including those who are monolingual in English and those without a background in teaching literature or language—can learn to (a) maintain and develop newcomer students' complex linguistic repertoires; (b) redefine teaching and learning as reciprocal, shared endeavors; and (c) gain practice creating opportunities for students to experiment with language in both informal and academic settings. In doing so, we seek to shift both educators' and students' approach to languaging, agency, and authority in the classroom, thus resocializing them to build collaborative and radically inclusive educational communities.

When working with newcomer and emergent plurilingual students, we often begin by asking three questions: Who are you?, who are we as a community? and what can we learn together? In *Radically Inclusive Teaching With Newcomer and Emergent Plurilingual Students: Braving Up*, we direct those questions to educators themselves: Who are we? Who are our students? What can we learn together? In the pages that follow, we invite you to join us in this exploration, using classroom vignettes, pedagogical strategies, and student stories to illustrate ways educators can bravely enact curricular, pedagogical, and policy shifts that transform the classroom and enhance the educational experiences of their students.

Radically Inclusive Teaching With Newcomer and Emergent Plurilingual Students: Braving Up consists of three parts. In Part I (Chapters 2 and 3), we establish a conceptual foundation for our work with newcomer and emergent plurilingual students, focusing on both the historical and political context of language education in the United States as well as structural aspects of our Language Explorer programs. In Part II, we step into classrooms, focusing on how educators use radically inclusive pedagogies to build community, scaffold literacy, and amplify students' plurilingual voices. This section of the book draws examples from a wide array of Language Explorer programs, including those offered over the summer, throughout the academic year, and, in response to the COVID-19 pandemic, online. Throughout, we feature examples of newcomer and emergent plurilingual students' writing, artwork, and analysis, inviting readers to learn with and from the voices, perspectives, and insights of students. Chapter 4 features curriculum and insight from teachers of multiple academic disciplines as we examine how educators scaffold student engagement and nourish brave, heteroglossic classrooms in which plurilingual students can thrive. In Chapter 5, we explore arts-based and plurilingual pedagogies, focusing on ways educators support and stretch students' analysis—and creation—of plurilingual poetic, narrative, and artistic analyses of social, linguistic, and literary borders. In Chapter 6, we focus on ways newcomer students leverage their plurilingual voices within and beyond the classroom, asking how educators and districts can learn from, and evolve in response to, students' insight. Chapter 7 highlights the opportunities and tensions that emerge when crises—such as the COVID-19 pandemic—force dramatic changes in schooling. In it, we explore the experiences of newcomer and emergent plurilingual students in online and virtual classrooms, and we consider enactments of humanizing, culturally and linguistically sustaining, teaching in online classrooms. In Part III, we shift our gaze beyond the classroom, considering what braving up means for educational systems and structures. In Chapter 8, we analyze implications for assessment and evaluation of students and educators, while Chapter 9 focuses on district-level programming and policy; this section includes case studies from one of our partner school districts, and draws on the expertise of guest co-author Renae Bryant, director of Plurilingual Services for Anaheim Union High School District.

WHAT DOES IT MEAN TO BE PROFICIENT?

One of the constructs that shapes approaches to language education in the United States is the concept of *proficiency*. The subject of innumerable standardized measures, language proficiency is often framed as the primary goal of districts' work with emergent plurilingual students; once students reach proficiency, they are "reclassified" and no longer subject to state oversight. It is as if once plurilingual students reach a specific point in their language development, their linguistic history ceases to exist and their linguistic future is not relevant.

This model is fundamentally at odds with the concept of culturally and linguistically sustaining teaching, which emphasizes the importance of engaging our students' full humanity: their histories, their cultures, their languaging; their passions, curiosities, and futures. It is also ideologically limiting; when we define our work as having a fixed and predetermined destination, we deny ourselves and our students the opportunity to grow in ways we have not yet imagined. As Vygotsky posited almost a century ago, thought and language are co-creating processes (1930/1962); thus, languaging is a dynamic process that evolves, adapts, and transforms as we interact and co-create communicative actions with others. While we appreciate the importance of assessing students' changing approach to languaging—not to mention our own successes as educators—it is important to recognize that we are all, always, "language learners" striving to stretch our linguistic repertoires and find deeper and more effective ways to communicate (see Chapter 8 for additional discussion of the concepts of proficiency and assessment).

In Figure 1.1, we present a developmental model that we find useful in our work with teachers and educational leaders: the cultural proficiency continuum (adapted from Lindsey, Nuri-Robins, Terrell, & Lindsey, 2018; see also Quezada, Rodríguez-Valls, & Lindsey, 2016). When introducing this model to educators, we challenge them to consider who they—and their districts—are today, and how they hope to grow in the future. This requires an act of critical reconciliation as we bravely and candidly assess our own vision, practice, and potential. Like climbing a staircase, braving up takes work, but also provides an opportunity to step into a radically different future.

The first three stages in this continuum are widely recognized as harmful; we rarely encounter educators who publicly self-identify as destructive, incapable, or evasive (though we do meet many who operate from these stances). During these stages of development, educational systems perceive newcomer and emergent plurilingual students as a problem to be solved in order to become compliant with political, fiscal, or academic imperatives related to equity and inclusion. In culturally destructive environments,

Figure 1.1. Cultural Proficiency Continuum

The Cultural Proficiency Continuum

Cultural Destructiveness

Cultural Incapacity

Cultural Evasion

Cultural Pre-competence

Cultural Competence

Cultural Proficiency

TRANSFORMATION FOR EQUITY

COMPLIANCE-BASED TOLERANCE FOR DIVERSITY

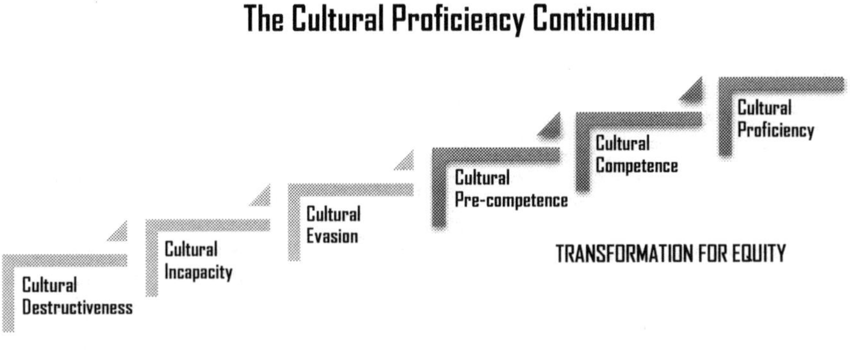

Adapted from Lindsey et al. (2018). Braving up begins as educators have the courage to move from pre-competence to proficiency and beyond.

educators actively suppress the identities and assets that students bring to their classrooms through English-only mandates and other assimilationist policies (such as those restricting students' dress, hairstyle, or other expression of identity). In the second developmental stage (cultural incapacity), educators and systems may not overtly prohibit students from expressing their cultural and linguistic identities, but rather frame them as wrong or less desirable (i.e., through culturally dominant definitions of "appropriate" or "respectful" behavior, or the hyperregulation of students' use of "standard" and "correct" grammar). Whereas destruction and incapacity refer to active and explicit actions, the third stage (cultural evasion) refers to the passive and implicit behaviors that emerge from educators' inability to see students as possessing cultural and linguistic resources. During this stage of development, educators often claim they want to help students "overcome their deficits" (i.e., their home lives or linguistic background) but fail to see, or discount, the assets that newcomer and emergent plurilingual students bring to the school community. We explore characteristics associated with these first three stages in greater depth in Chapter 2, as we examine the ideological underpinnings of deficit-based educational policies.

We anticipate that most readers of this book, however, would locate themselves on the right half of the continuum, having already begun the work of braving up and striving toward transformation. At the precompetence level, educators are becoming aware of and acknowledging that there is much they don't yet know. This is the beginning of true curiosity about newcomer and emergent plurilingual students, and it is marked by the posing of questions about who students are and how to better engage, affirm, and support. We think of pre-competence as the beginning of educators' journey toward radically inclusive teaching, the moment at which they become willing to push themselves and open up to the possibility of learning from their students.

Cultural competence suggests an increasing ability to use our learning to benefit students. Culturally competent teachers see value in the heterogeneity of culture, language, and ideas, and have the ability to change and evolve in response to that heterogeneity. This stage is characterized by shifts in curriculum and pedagogy as educators strive to better engage, affirm, and amplify students' cultural and linguistic identities, passions, and epistemologies. As educators take steps toward proficiency, they look beyond individual classrooms and engage broader questions of policy and practice. Just as educators in a stage of pre-competence are ready to begin their journey, as educators and systems develop cultural proficiency, they are poised for transformation. That is the place where the work of radically inclusive teaching begins.

WHO ARE WE?

Alison was raised White and monolingual in a suburban school district in Long Island, New York. Though Alison's own family was decidedly working-class, the school district she attended was notable for its wealth, high test scores, and overwhelming Whiteness: when Alison graduated from high school, 97% of the residents of her town self-identified as white (United States Census Bureau, 1990). Like Alison, many of her classmates were second- or third-generation Americans whose Greek, Italian, or Jewish heritage was expressed primarily through foods, family gatherings, and school-sponsored "multicultural day" celebrations. Students had a strong sense of ethnic pride, but assimilation was prized; you wanted to be ethnic enough to fit in, but never come across as anything other than wholly "American." Every one of the some 25 teachers Alison encountered in grades K–12 was White, and the only time she heard a language other than English spoken at school was in Spanish class. For Alison, adolescence and young adulthood were a time of dislocation and disconnect; despite sharing racial and linguistic markers with her peers, her queerness and lived experiences rendered her irreparably different. The duality she experienced while navigating intractable manifestations of privilege and oppression is what led her to work for justice.

By contrast, Ferran grew up in Barcelona, Catalunya/Spain during the last years of a fascist dictatorship regime. His home language was Catalán. At the school he attended, Catalán was neither the language of instruction nor a subject part of the curriculum. The first time Catalán was part of Ferran's "academic" education was at the Universitat de Barcelona. There, he walked his first steps as an educator. Later, he moved to California, where he worked in a school district south of the City of Angels. Learning with and working with Latinx students, he completely deconstructed his stance as plurilingual educator; the way he designed teaching and learning by including the students' linguistic repertoires; and most importantly, he shifted his practices as an *adalid* (guide) of teaching language to become an educator committed to co-construct just, equitable, and inclusive languaging spaces.

It was from these roots that we began our journeys into the world of education. In the decades before we met, we traveled very different paths. Alison describes herself as an "activist first"; teaching was something she fell into from the world of equity-oriented community and youth leadership work. Officially, Alison was an English Language Arts teacher and holds a doctorate in social justice education; unofficially, she uses those credentials to gain access to institutional spaces in order to support young people—and educators—in leveraging their positionality, voices, and agency to promote justice. For Ferran, his journey took him to teach Catalán to immigrant students from North Africa who made Catalunya their home. Following this experience and as he moved to California, he had to rethink the validity of his languaging practices. His knowledge of the named language Spanish was a colonizing tool in need of a transformation. One step at a time (and still a work in progress), his linguistic repertoire puzzled with different named languages as Ferran became a plurilingual being who is capable of developing a collective classroom discourse with his students.

By 2016, our careers had brought us both to California State University, Fullerton, where we discovered a shared passion for supporting young people in using their voices to explore, critique, and co-create educational spaces. We approach this work through somewhat different lenses: Ferran's expertise is in challenging monolingualism and coaching students and teachers as they creatively stretch their linguistic repertoires, whereas Alison's centers enactments of agency, emergent curriculum, and teaching for social justice. Those linguistic, ideological, pedagogical, and political emphases shape every aspect of our work, as we continually ask ourselves, each other, and the educators with whom we work: Where will you stretch? How will you use your power? What do you need to grow?

WHAT CAN WE LEARN TOGETHER?

This book is written as a professional conversation, not a lecture. Transforming ourselves and our systems requires critical reflection, courage, and action; all of these are best done in community. As you explore the vignettes, examples, and challenges from teachers, educational leaders, and newcomer students themselves, we invite you to read, critique, and talk back to them. What do you notice? What are you wondering? What can you learn?

Each chapter of *Radically Inclusive Teaching With Newcomer and Emergent Plurilingual Students: Braving Up* closes with questions for professional learning and reflection. These are designed to support individual and teams of educators in critically reflecting on their own educational contexts and considering their next steps toward transformation. We encourage readers to use these questions to spark conversation at the school-site level, and we include additional readings and resources for professional learning on our companion website at www.bravingup.com and via Teachers College Press at tcpress.com/dover-resources. The first of these is a glossary; we invite you to use this resource as you turn the page, stretch your linguistic repertoire, and join us in braving up.

If I Were to Change the World, by Gurpreet Mangat

BY : GURPREET MANGAT

If I were to change the world,
I'd cancel crimes
I'd cancel the war
I'd even cancel ਹਿੰਸਕ ਵਿਰੋਧ. (violent protests).

If I were in charge of the world,
There would be no homeless people.
There would be no judgment by my appearance.
There would even be ਕੋਈ ਨਸਲ, ਕੋਈ ਦੇਸ਼ ਨਹੀਂ, ਇੱਕ
ਧਰਤੀ ਹੋਵੇਗੀ ਜਿੱਥੇ ਸਾਰੇ ਲੋਕ ਇਕੱਠੇ ਰਹਿੰਦੇ ਹਨ. (no race, no
countries, there will be only human beings where
they live together.)

If I were in charge of the world
You wouldn't ਸੌਣ ਦਾ ਸਮਾਂ ਹੈ (have bedtimes,)
You wouldn't have adults driving.
You wouldn't have any sickness.
You wouldn't ਇਥੋਂ ਤਕ ਕੰਮ(even have chores.)

If I were in charge of the world
And a person who forgot to take a shower.
And sometimes ਆਪਣੀਆਂ ਜੁੱਤੀਆਂ ਬੰਨਣਾ ਭੁੱਲ ਗਏ((forgot
to tie their shoes.)
Would still be allowed to be
In charge of the world.

Part I

FOUNDATIONS

CHAPTER 2

The Ground on Which We Stand: Conceptual Foundations for Braving Up

Ten years after García, Kleifgen, and Falchi (2008) wrote "One of the most misunderstood issues in pre-K–12 education today is how to educate children who are not yet proficient in English" (p. 6), school districts across the country continue to struggle to find effective ways to work with and learn from newcomer students and families. Instead of amplifying emergent bi- and plurilingual students' already expansive linguistic resources, schools routinely frame newcomer students as "English Learners" who lack the communicative skills to fully participate in academic settings.

For example, during a recent meeting, a school superintendent told us about visiting an elementary school where newcomer students were isolated for pullout language remediation. Rather than building community with fellow students and teachers, newcomer students were seated alone in hallways listening to audio recordings in English; they were linguistically and socially isolated, and teachers did not know how to engage them in the classroom. "You can see the impact on students," the school superintendent said. "They are pulling out their hair, missing school due to stress. It's not what we want for them, and everyone knows it doesn't work. But we don't have anything else to offer." This book is written for teachers and administrators like this one, who see a problem in how they currently engage newcomer students and are looking for new ways to approach newcomer and multilingual education.

THE POWER OF LANGUAGING

Despite all the research conducted over the last 4 decades (Cummins, 1979; De Jong & Howard, 2009; Delpit, 2006, 2009; Krashen, 1985; Lindholm-Leary & Hernández, 2011; Tarone & Swain, 1995; Valdés, 2015) that attests to the importance of affirming students' full linguistic repertoires, as well as legislation—such as Proposition 58,[2] Global California 2030, and the State Seal of Biliteracy in California—that explicitly values plurilingualism, many educational agencies continue to use deficit labels such as English Learners (ELs) to identify and classify students. Labels like these fail to acknowledge that newcomer and emergent plurilingual students enter classrooms with a robust and dynamic *linguistic repertoire* that encompasses a wide array of verbal and nonverbal markers. In our work, we define linguistic repertoire as an evolving tool that includes all the registers, idiolects, nuances, and variances that someone uses when communicating orally, in writing, or nonverbally. As students explore and experiment with multiple languages, they stretch and expand their linguistic repertoires, and develop the ability to access "different linguistic features or various modes . . . as autonomous languages, in order to maximize communicative potential" (García, 2009, p. 140).

Labels like English Learner presuppose that newcomer and emergent plurilingual students are half-empty vessels that need to be filled with "English Language Skills" (Hernandez, 2017; Shapiro, 2014; Shin 2017). That perspective leads to practices like those described by the superintendent quoted above. In our work with teachers and administrators, we challenge them to position newcomer students as Emergent Plurilingual (EP) students, who enter our classrooms with unique and expanding linguistic repertoires that are ready to be utilized as classroom resources; in fact, most students whom districts label as ELs are actually already *plurilingual,* in that they have the ability to use multiple languages at varying levels of proficiency and for different purposes (Council of Europe, 2007). Our challenge, then, is not to address students' "deficits," but to figure out how to support all students—including monolingual and plurilingual students—in exploring, playing with, and using their linguistic repertoires as a bridge to complex disciplinary content.

BRAVING UP: STRETCHING OUR PRACTICE

The phrase *braving up* comes from a teacher, Tadea,[3] with whom we worked during one of our newcomer programs. She was talking about her students and how she saw them beginning to open up and experiment with language:

> I was awestruck when I saw the level of detail they included in their writing. They all opened up and explained to us the struggles they are facing, and it really painted an emotional picture in my mind. These kids are braving up, and I love that. (Dover & Rodríguez-Valls, 2018, p. 67)

Being a newcomer student does require bravery. Newcomer students are, by definition, in entirely unfamiliar settings populated by people who do not speak their language. As described in Chapter 1, newcomer students in the United States are frequently emerging from periods of significant migrancy, political strife, and personal trauma; they may enter school sites grieving family, community, and cultural networks from their country of origin. Simply showing up for school each day is testament to newcomers' extraordinary bravery and commitment to their academic growth. In Part II, we explore some of the pedagogical strategies teachers can use to nourish "brave spaces" (Arao & Clemens, 2013) where newcomer and emergent bilingual students can build community, share their stories, and participate fully in academic discourse.

However, what struck us about Tadea's comment was the bravery that she and her fellow teachers also demonstrated. Radically inclusive teaching requires new and veteran educators—as well as students—to step out of their own comfort zones, to brave up as they learn to explore, question, and expand their own linguistic and professional practices. It also requires educational communities to reconsider the ways we conceptualize linguistic practices in schools and to challenge some of the assumptions that undergird our pedagogy.

FROM LANGUAGE TO LANGUAGING: ADOPTING A HETEROGLOSSIC IDEOLOGY

One of the assumptions that creates a barrier for newcomer and emergent plurilingual students is the prevalence of a monoglossic language ideology, or the belief that language is a discrete skill that can be isolated and divorced from its context (García & Torres-Guevara, 2009). This ideology underlies constructions like "home language" and "school language," or "L1" and "L2," as if students' experiences of language can be isolated and experienced independently. This mindset, which is pervasive within U.S. public education, is grounded in the assumptions that (a) languages are static, discrete, and immutable systems (rather than socially constructed agreements), and (b) using multiple languages concurrently is wrong. This belief system fails to reflect the increasingly complex linguistic structures present in many plurilingual communities, in which members incorporate and adapt features of multiple languages concurrently and for different purposes. It is worth noting that while not exclusive to the United States, monolinguistic ideologies are especially pervasive here in comparison to other regions, such as Europe, where official language policies have historically valued plurilingualism as a core component of citizenship. In establishing goals for language education throughout Europe, for example, the Council of Europe (2007) noted that

> The development of plurilingualism is not simply a functional necessity: it is also an essential component of democratic behaviour. Recognition of the diversity of speakers' plurilingual repertoires should lead to acceptance of linguistic differences: respect for the linguistic rights of individuals and groups in their relations with the state and linguistic majorities, respect for freedom of expression, respect for linguistic minorities, respect for the least commonly spoken and taught national languages, respect for language diversity in interregional and international communication. Language education policies are intimately connected with education in the values of democratic citizenship because their purposes are complementary: language teaching, the ideal locus for intercultural contact, is a sector in which education for democratic life in its intercultural dimensions can be included in education systems. (p. 36)

At the same time that the Council of Europe was establishing policies encouraging plurilingualism, monolingualism (under the guise of English proficiency) continued to be a driving factor within U.S. education policy; this monoglossic ideology was evident not only through "English-only" mandates, but also the teaching of "foreign languages" and labeling of "English Learners." Thus, in his analysis of next steps for language activism, Pennycook (2019) argues that educators must avoid "demolinguistic labels" (p. 170) that characterize students according to the named languages they do or do not speak (e.g., terms like *English Learner* and *Spanish speaker*) and instead leverage the situated advantages associated with students' multifaceted and dynamic cultural, social, and linguistic identities and practices. Pennycook notes that

> These resources are not only linguistic but multimodal: students may employ a complex array of resources in their learning and, as educators, we need to be wary of that trap that links learning only to forms of language and literacy with which we may be familiar. (p. 170)

It is not uncommon for bi- or plurilingual people, media, and texts to draw from multiple discursive and linguistic practices, a practice that is often called translanguaging (Flores & García, 2013). Translanguaging theory is based on the idea that the distinctions among named languages are social constructs: while our societies dictate—and enforce—which words and discursive patterns comprise "English" and "Farsi," for example, in practice, plurilingual people consciously or unconsciously draw from their full knowledge of language whenever they communicate. Basaran's (2017) depiction of the mental processes of multilingual people (see Figure 2.1) provides an especially effective visual representation of the difference between bilingual models of language development and translanguaging theory; in it we see learners pulling from their full linguistic repertoires rather than disrupting their cognitive processes based upon socially constructed language boundaries.

Monoglossic ideologies lead educators to shut down students' use of multiple languages, encouraging them to "focus on English," rather than consciously stretch their linguistic repertoires by making connections between their existing linguistic structures and new content and concepts. While few educators with a monoglossic ideology see themselves as oppressive, monoglossia reflects the colonial, assimilationist roots of U.S. public education, in which being monocultural and monolingual (in English) has historically been positioned as more desirable than multicultural and plurilingual identities. This is sometimes referred to as one of the ways "White gaze" shapes educational and linguistic policies and practices, irrespective of the racial and linguistic identities of educators and students themselves (Flores & Rosa, 2015).

By contrast, *heteroglossic ideologies* recognize that bi- and plurilingual students' multiple language registers coexist and enrich each other (Flores &

Figure 2.1. Translanguaging (Basaran, 2017)

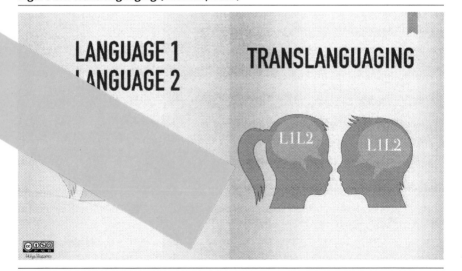

Source: Image copyright Hülya Basaran, available at https://frokenhulya.wordpress.com /2017/10/12/translanguaging-flersprakighet-som-resurs/bli110-001/. CC-BY-NC-SA.

Schissel, 2014; Kiramba, 2019; Krulatz & Iversen, 2020; Solsona-Puig, Capdevila-Gutiérrez, & Rodríguez-Valls, 2018). For plurilingual students, languages are interactive and complementary, and intrinsically dependent upon one another, suggesting teachers must find ways to embrace and engage plurilingual students' full linguistic repertoires as they teach subject area content and literacy. Thus, emergent plurilingual students' linguistic repertoires are not empty vessels awaiting English, but instead an intrinsic tool teachers can draw upon as they cocreate a "shared lifeworld" that is "bounded by the totality of interpretations presupposed by [students'] background knowledge" (Habermas 1981/1987, p. 13).

Flores and García (2013) describe the shift toward heteroglossic ideology as the adoption of a *translanguaging stance,* where educators invite and embrace students' multiple languages, model linguistic fluidity and risk-taking, and function as linguistic co-learners alongside students. See Chapter 3 for additional discussion of how we coach educators in exploring and developing their translanguaging stance, as well as Part II for examples of what this looks like in the classroom.

CHALLENGING LINGUISTIC DOMINANCE

Before educational communities can brave up and build heteroglossic spaces, we must acknowledge the systemic factors that impact language development and the prospect of bilingualism and plurilingualism for students of color and historically minoritized and marginalized students. These include educators' perceptions and judgments about the multidimensionality of emergent plurilingual students' linguistic repertoires, and the intersectionality of race and language.

In the United States, students identified as newcomer, English Learner, and/or emergent plurilingual are overwhelmingly students of color (U.S. Department of Education, 2015). This creates a system whereby students who are "native speakers of English" tend to have other social and political privileges, including parental access to English-speaking administrators, teachers, and stakeholders; citizenship; socioeconomic resources; and encouragement to learn a second language as an opportunity for enrichment. By contrast, the linguistic repertoires of students of color and of historically minoritized and marginalized students are routinely positioned as less valuable than the linguistic repertoires of English-speaking (White) students (Flores & Rosa, 2019). Essentially, English-speaking students are encouraged to become plurilingual as a form of enrichment, whereas students of color experience a subtractive model where they are pressured to "learn to read and write the dominant language [English] at the expense of developing native language literacy" (Bussert-Webb, Masso, & Lewis, 2018, p. 2649).

The standardization of English as the linguistic benchmark has created labels such as *Standard English Learner* (SEL). SEL students, as defined within the California English Language Arts/English Language Development framework (California Department of Education, 2015), are

> native speakers of English who are ethnic minority students (e.g., African American, American Indian, Southeast Asian American, Mexican American, Native Pacific Islander) and whose mastery of the standard English language privileged in schools is limited because they use an ethnic-specific nonstandard dialect of English in their homes and communities and use Standard English in limited ways. (p. 882)

Rosa (2018) explains how this idea of limited language proficiency permeates to labels such as Long-Term English Learner (LTEL) and Heritage Language Learner (HLL), among others. The label Limited Language Proficiency in English (LEP) diminishes the multidimensionality of plurilingual students' linguistic repertoires. García & Tupas (2018) forewarn us that "the bilingualism of indigenous, conquered, refugee, or immigrant youth is often perceived as a problem" (p. 391), instead of one of the many assets they bring to school communities. This type of "deficit bilingualism" is among the most pervasive ideologies in U.S. public education and serves as the driving force behind English-only legislation, which at its peak in the early 21st century led to the disruption of bilingual and dual-language programs nationwide.

Under deficit bilingualism, English is situated as the "lingua franca" (Hemphill & Blakely, 2019, p. 221), or the primary and most privileged language in linguistically diverse spaces. The road from primacy to dominance is short, and deficit bilingualism is grounded in supremacist presumption that a) native fluency in English is the most important goal, and b) any knowledge and competency on other languages creates an obstacle for students' development as "native/standardized" English speakers (Tochon, 2019). Although English-only policies have been repealed in many states throughout the country, their impact continues to resonate; it is not uncommon for plurilingual teachers and students alike to silence themselves in response to dominant epistemologies regarding what academic conversation "should" be (for additional analyses of linguistic insecurity, see Baldaquí Escandell, 2009; Ek, Sánchez, & Quijada Cerecer, 2013).

Just as antiracist teaching requires educators to acknowledge the myriad ways White supremacy has shaped U.S. educational policy and practice

Figure 2.2. Using Poetry to Critique Language Policy

Acclaimed poet Martín Espada wrote this poem as a critique of English-only mandates in Lynn, Massachusetts. To hear Espada read and introduce his poem, visit https://voca.arizona.edu/readings-list/535/1022.

The New Bathroom Policy at English High School

Nueva Norma Para el Baño en la English High School
by Martín Espada
The boys chatter Spanish
from the bathroom
while the principal
listens from his stall
The only word he recognizes
is his own name
and this constipates him
So he decides
to ban Spanish
from the bathrooms
Now he can relax

Source: Espada, M. (1990). *Rebellion Is the Circle of a Lover's Hands.* Curbstone Press. Reprinted with permission.

(Bonilla-Silva, 2006; Kohli, 2021; Matias & Mackey, 2016; Picower, 2021; Sleeter, 2001), so too must educators grapple with the complex and pervasive impact of monoglossia and monolingualism in the classroom. In addition to analyzing the ideological and practical impact of languaging policy and practice within their school sites, braving up requires educators to reconsider their *own* approach to languaging and reimagine their classroom as a space of linguistic experimentation and affirmation. Figure 2.2 provides one such example; in a poem that was a favorite among Alison's predominantly Puerto Rican students in Central Massachusetts, poet Martín Espada challenges the English-only movement in a nearby district.

Thus, in the chapters to come, we focus not on how to better teach "English Language Development," but rather on how educational systems can enact linguistically inclusive, plurilingual pedagogies that

- stretch the interconnectedness of all the variances, codes, and registers students already possess in their linguistic repertoires;
- empower students to fully use their [trans]languaging skills;

- challenge and expand the idea of what constitutes "academic language" and classroom discourse; and
- provide opportunities for students and teachers to explore, experiment with, and stretch their linguistic repertoires.

CENTERING CULTURALLY AND LINGUISTICALLY SUSTAINING PEDAGOGY

Overall, we position our work with newcomer and emergent plurilingual students as part of a broader effort to enact culturally and linguistically sustaining curriculum, pedagogy, and policy. Informed by the work of Paris (2012) and Paris and Alim (2017), who define culturally sustaining pedagogy as teaching that "seeks to perpetuate and foster—to sustain—linguistic, literate, and cultural pluralism as part of the democratic project of schooling" (Paris, 2012, p. 93), we seek to consciously interrupt educational processes that marginalize or "other" newcomer and emergent plurilingual students.

In the chapters that follow, we explore how the use of culturally relevant (Ladson-Billings, 1995) and responsive pedagogy (Gay, 2000) can help educational communities reconceptualize teaching and learning within a liberatory third space (Gutiérrez, 2008) that nourishes multilingual, multicultural, and radically inclusive teaching and learning. In so doing, we ground our thinking in the concept of emergent curriculum (Dover & Schultz, 2018), wherein students themselves not only shape and define the boundaries of learning, but in which students' lives become the narratives we explore in the classroom. Throughout, we ask questions like those in Figure 2.3, which consider how educators might "turn toward students" as they challenge normative practices and hierarchical relationships in their classrooms.

As we highlight the types of curricular, pedagogical, and programmatic shifts that can interrupt the marginalization and exclusion of newcomer and emergent plurilingual students, we wish to be explicit: these are not recommended "modifications" to normative educational practices. Instead, we wish to highlight the tremendous opportunities that arise when educators brave up and nourish educational spaces that celebrate, learn from, and inspire learning among culturally, linguistically, and experientially diverse students.

Thus, braving up is not a set of strategies, but rather a conscious and strategic revisioning of the concept of good teaching. In the chapters that follow, we explore the pedagogic and political actions that comprise our work, which we explicitly position as an act of teaching for social justice (see Dover, 2013, 2015, 2016) intended to disrupt oppressive educational discourse and policy, and reimagine schooling as inherently bound to our individual and collective humanity.

Figure 2.3. Student-Centered Teaching in Action

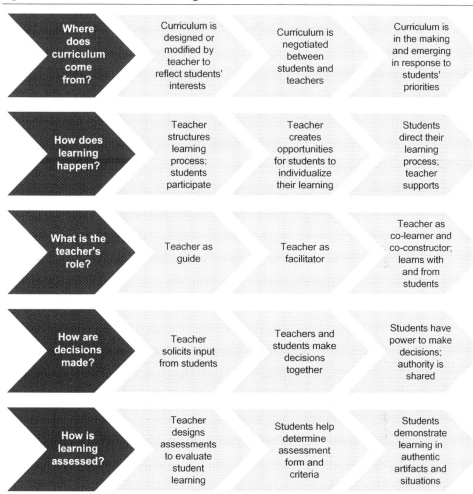

Where does curriculum come from?	Curriculum is designed or modified by teacher to reflect students' interests	Curriculum is negotiated between students and teachers	Curriculum is in the making and emerging in response to students' priorities
How does learning happen?	Teacher structures learning process; students participate	Teacher creates opportunities for students to individualize their learning	Students direct their learning process; teacher supports
What is the teacher's role?	Teacher as guide	Teacher as facilitator	Teacher as co-learner and co-constructor; learns with and from students
How are decisions made?	Teacher solicits input from students	Teachers and students make decisions together	Students have power to make decisions; authority is shared
How is learning assessed?	Teacher designs assessments to evaluate student learning	Students help determine assessment form and criteria	Students demonstrate learning in authentic artifacts and situations

Source: Dover & Schultz (2018, p. 207). Reprinted with permission.

Resources and Reflective Activities for Chapter 2

- This chapter features the following quote from the Council of Europe (2007):

> The development of plurilingualism is not simply a functional necessity: it is also an essential component of democratic behaviour. Recognition of the diversity of speakers' plurilingual repertoires should lead to

> acceptance of linguistic differences: respect for the linguistic rights of individuals and groups in their relations with the state and linguistic majorities, respect for freedom of expression, respect for linguistic minorities, respect for the least commonly spoken and taught national languages, respect for language diversity in inter-regional and international communication. Language education policies are intimately connected with education in the values of democratic citizenship because their purposes are complementary: language teaching, the ideal locus for intercultural contact, is a sector in which education for democratic life in its intercultural dimensions can be included in education systems. (p. 36)

- How does this vision compare to the ways mono-, bi-, multi-, and plurilingualism are defined and function within your own educational context? How do the language education policies in your school, district, and state reflect—or fail to reflect—this interpretation of democracy?
- Where do you see terms like *Standard English* or *academic language* used in your own educational context? Are there norms, policies, or assessment practices that privilege speakers of dominant linguistic registers? See the companion website for additional readings related to manifestations of linguistic dominance in schools.
- In Figure 2.3, Dover and Schultz (2018) offer a series of continua depicting ways educators might shift from "centering" students to "co-constructing" teaching and learning. Where would you place yourself on these continua? Your colleagues? Do your responses change as you consider your approach to teaching newcomer and emergent plurilingual students versus students labeled as "English proficient" or considered academically elite? Why?
- Additional resources can be found at www.bravingup.com and at Teachers College Press at tcpress.com/dover-resources.

CHAPTER 3

"This Is How School Should Be!": Learning from the Language Explorers[4]

The examples and classroom vignettes presented in this book come from our experience developing, implementing, and overseeing district-based programming for newcomer and emergent plurilingual students in Southern California. These include migrant education programs as well as our summer and academic year Language Explorer enrichment programs for newcomer students. Overall, our goal is not to offer remedial programs for "English Learners," but to nourish inclusive, academically robust, and fun-learning experiences that provide opportunities for historically marginalized and minoritized young people—and their teachers—to disrupt institutional rhetoric regarding newcomer and emergent bilingual students. Specifically, we seek to value, validate, and vindicate newcomer and emergent plurilingual students by cultivating a pedagogic voice that "constantly and intelligently stands up against injustice and does so from a culturally and community-anchored standpoint" (Valenzuela, 2016, p. 5).

Among the most powerful strands of our work is the collaboration between our university, California State University, Fullerton, and partner school districts throughout Southern California to offer a monthlong summer enrichment experience for newcomer, refugee, immigrant, and emergent plurilingual students entering grades 7 through 12. Since 2015, our Language Explorer programs have engaged some 700 newcomer students and 80 pre- and in-service educators from three school districts in arts-based, (multi)literacy-rich explorations of identity, culture, and languaging in poetry, film, graphic novels, young adult literature, and their own lives. Participating students come from more than 23 countries and 19 linguistic communities and have diverse linguistic proficiencies; it is not unusual for a class of 20 students to include members of 5–7 different language groups, with U.S. residency ranging from scant weeks to as long as 2 years. The program has brought widespread local and national recognition to participating teachers, students, and districts: Anaheim Union High School District's

Summer Language Academy, for example, won both the 2018 Orange County Department of Education Cultural and Linguistic Responsiveness Award and the 2019 Golden Bell Award from the California School Boards Association, and educators from multiple program sites have joined us in presenting their work at national and international conferences.

In recent years, we have expanded beyond a summer intensive program to create academic year and Saturday programs that provide continuity and community for newcomer and emergent plurilingual students; our teachers also bring aspects of the Language Explorers curriculum and pedagogy into their daily work as teachers of mathematics, science, humanities, and language development. This wraparound approach ensures that newcomer and emergent plurilingual students are served not only in specialized enrichment programs, but also throughout the academic year; it also positioned teachers to respond effectively when the COVID-19 pandemic forced dramatic shifts in teaching and learning (see Chapter 7).

In each of our Language Explorer programs, we recast the classroom as a global village where identity and citizenship are multidimensional, transcultural, and plurilingual. In the monthlong Summer Language Academy (SLA), for example, teachers share their own cultural and linguistic journeys, emphasize that students' cultural identities and linguistic repertoires are assets, invite students to strategically leverage their multiple languages in oral and written presentations, and encourage students to draw connections figuratively and literally between their own experiences and those depicted in literature. While the curriculum changes each year, the overarching structure progresses from an exploration of self (answering questions like, "who are you?") to an exploration of our collective identity ("who are we?") as members of classroom, geographic, and human communities. See Chapters 4 through 7 for examples of what this exploration looks like in face-to-face and virtual classrooms, or visit the companion website at www .bravingup.com or Teachers College Press at tcpress.com/dover-resources to take a student-created virtual tour of the SLA.

At the beginning, we envisioned the SLA as an alternate environment in which teachers and students could function outside of a monoglossic, regimented educational system. Rather than reacting to test scores and standardized curriculum, they had the freedom to build learning communities that authentically responded to the unique, situated academic, cultural, and linguistic priorities of the learners in the classroom. This approach met with great success: over the course of just 16 days—48 instructional hours—teachers nourished learning communities in which newcomer students were able to share their stories, stretch their linguistic repertoires, and develop a sense of identity and agency as valued members of their school communities. In the process, pre- and in-service educators learned to create educational spaces that affirm, sustain, and foster academic achievement among culturally and linguistically diverse newcomer and emergent plurilingual students. As we have expanded our Language Explorer programs in recent years, we continue to think of our programs as opportunities for experimentation and professional learning, but also as critically important mechanisms for systemic transformation. That is, braving up does not only mean creating alternative, plurilingual spaces that evade restrictive policies and mandates, but actively using these spaces to reimagine what schooling can and should look like overall. Thus, we challenge readers to consider not only the Language Explorer programs as we enacted them, but how the ideologies, explorations, and pedagogies we describe manifest—or fail to manifest—in your own context. What does schooling look like in your own classroom, district, and community? And how can you stretch your own vision of what schooling could be?

Whenever we talk about our work with a new group of teachers or district administrators, they look at us with a combination of disbelief and awe. "How is that possible? How did you find teachers who speak all those languages?" they ask. Put simply, we don't. Each class of 20 students is staffed by a strategically selected three-member team of mono- and plurilingual preservice teachers, instructional assistants, and district teachers; generally, we aim to build instructional teams that represent three languages and draw from multiple disciplinary perspectives. Our teachers are not necessarily polyglots; instead, they are educators with a commitment to learning with and about emergent plurilingual and newcomer students, and trained in the principles and pedagogies of culturally and linguistically sustaining practice. They must be; unlike academic year programs, where teachers have months to establish classroom communities and cultivate student learning, in most of our programs we have just 48 hours. We must be strategic in our efforts; there is no time to lose.

In the remainder of this chapter, we provide a broad overview of the Language Explorers, introducing both the conceptual and pedagogical lenses that shape it as well as some of our student and teacher participants. Throughout, we invite readers to consider the multiple purposes of programming for newcomer and plurilingual students—from language attainment, to the development of inclusive school communities, to professional learning for educators—as well as the complexities of developing educational offerings that engage an ever-changing and culturally, linguistically, and experientially diverse community of students. In focusing on the SLA, we wish to highlight it as an example of one way we partner with school districts to create affirming educational spaces that function as "learning labs" where students and educators can brave up; take personal, professional, and pedagogic risks; and begin to reconceptualize what culturally and linguistically sustaining classrooms look like. Later in the book, we explore how teachers bring this approach into their daily academic year interactions with students (in Chapters 4 through 7), as well as recommendations for programmatic, professional learning, and administrative shifts that can foster radically inclusive classrooms (in Chapters 8 and 9). For now, however, we invite you to join us as we step into the SLA.

DAY ONE: HOW IT BEGINS

The doors open to reveal semi-decorated classrooms. Empty bulletin boards are punctuated by an eclectic assortment of artifacts—puzzle pieces, name tags, and micrographies[5]—tentatively created by teachers in the hopes of modeling, inviting, and inspiring students to share of themselves. Graphic novels and children's books lie motionless on tables, awaiting the hands and ideas of those who will give them new meaning.

Students begin to trickle in, one by one. It is 8:30 a.m. on a Monday in June, and the silence is deafening. Students look around, wondering, who can understand me here? They meet the eyes of a teacher or student, or avert their eyes to avoid being seen. As they glance around the room, they pause when they encounter the word "welcome" written in 12 languages. They find their own and release a breath. It will be different here.

An hour passes, and drops of ink begin to color the empty pages of newly owned notebooks. Unfinished sentences and single words in Arabic, Vietnamese, Spanish, Korean, and English speak to the hesitation, diversity, and tentative engagement emanating from each seat. As midmorning approaches, desks are no longer anonymous; they have been named by those who for the next 15 days will read, write, talk, sing, share, critique, and present in this space.

After a short respite in the courtyard outside the classroom, a prompt appears on the whiteboard: "Who are you? Describe in the language of your choice anything and everything about you. You have 45 minutes, so take your time." The prompt is simple in its phrasing but complex in its depth, designed to create a foundation for a community of explorers who want and need to *confiar* (trust) each other. Pens are frozen, wondering if they have something to say. Questioning the why and the honesty of the prompt; whispering, do they really want to know who I am? Do I know who I am?

As noon approaches, a pile of responses emerges on the central table. Some papers have thorough descriptions, others claim shyness, and a few are too scant to qualify as responses at all. As the door closes on the first day, it is clear the group is not yet sure how to answer such an intimate question. Nevertheless, tiny sparkles of *esperanza* (hope) flicker as students walk in pairs and triads out the door; this group, it is becoming.

THE MONTHS BEFORE: WHEN IT *REALLY* BEGINS

The success of the Language Explorer programs reinforces what research highlights: the importance of culturally and linguistically responsive, (multi)literacy-rich instruction that invites and validates the cultural and linguistic experience of newcomer/new Americans (Creese & Blackledge, 2010; Genesee, Lindholm-Leary, Saunders, & Christian, 2005). When students learn with educators who have strong understandings of culturally and linguistically responsive pedagogy, they tend to develop a deeper sense of their own identity, which is correlated with higher levels of academic performance (Borrero & Sanchez, 2017; Lopez, 2016). By building an educational space where educators and students are taught to value what each participant brings to the classroom, we can create a "Zone of Cultural Comfort" (Rodríguez-Valls, 2009) in which each community member assumes the role of a knowledgeable other (Vygotsky, 1930/1962) who supports others in deepening their cultural and linguistic awareness.

Conceptually, our work is grounded in theories and practices of *translanguaging* (see Chapter 2), in which educators embrace the literacies and discursive practices of multiple languages, model linguistic fluidity and risk-taking, and function as linguistic co-learners alongside their students (Flores & García, 2013). García and Seltzer (2016) define translanguaging pedagogy as "the strategic deployment of a speaker's full linguistic repertoire to learn and develop their language repertoire and at the same time work toward social justice by equalizing positions of learners" (p. 23). The *-ing* is intended to highlight the dynamic nature of language: that language is constantly in flux and best described by the ways it is used; it is not something to be artificially bordered and tightly regulated.

For many of the educators who staff the SLA, this is a new concept. Translanguaging (as a term) saw its first usage in 1994, when Cen Williams, a Welsh researcher, used the Welsh word *trawsieithu* to describe bilingual pedagogy in Welsh/English classrooms (Vogel & García, 2017). In a Vygotskian example of thought and language emerging as co-creating processes (1930/1962), a field has rapidly grown around the term; as of July 2021, more than 21,000 articles on translanguaging have been published. Ofelia García of the City University of New York has emerged as among the most influential leaders in the field; her work with the CUNY-NYS Initiative on Emergent Bilinguals (https://www.cuny-nysieb.org/) is arguably the most important research related to language education and policy in decades.

Given the relatively recent emergence of translanguaging as a field, it is unsurprising that many educators are unfamiliar with the concept. It is at odds with historic approaches to bilingual education, which generally advocated discrete, diglossic (separated and independent) language systems. Some of these approaches, such as sink-or-swim approaches to English immersion and 50/50 models of bilingual education (where students spend half of the day learning exclusively in one language and half of the day learning in another), can result in "double monolingualism" rather than biliteracy; they create barriers within students' linguistic systems, and deny them opportunities to utilize their full linguistic repertoires and identities (Lippi-Green, 2011). This isolation of languages is at odds with translanguaging, which seeks to create a social and educational space where multilingual students can bring together "different dimensions of their personal history, experience and environment, their attitude, belief and ideology, their physical and cognitive capacity into one coordinated and meaningful experience" (Wei, 2011, p. 1223).

There are also educators who misinterpret translanguaging as *code-switching*, an approach that defines language categories as discrete and disconnected, but highlights the ways plurilingual speakers move among them (see Vogel & García, 2017). While we see much value in bilingual and dual-language education programs, as well as the importance of teaching students how to code-switch in response to social, professional, and academic demands, these cognitive models are functionally different from how we frame the languaging practices of our newcomer students. Thus, we begin our work by coaching educators in adopting a "translanguaging stance" (Flores & García, 2013) as they explore languaging practices, first in their own lives and stories, then in literature, and finally in the classroom. In so doing, we seek to not only challenge monolingualism and monoglossic ideologies, but to do so as a part of a broader effort toward racial, linguistic, and social justice, an approach increasingly referred to as a critical translingual approach (de los Ríos, Seltzer, & Molina, 2021; Seltzer, 2020).

GETTING READY: BUILDING OUR FOUNDATION

As university-based researchers and teacher educators, we see our role not as providing "professional development" per se, but rather as collaborating with school-based educators to reimagine what it means to teach and learn in radically inclusive, plurilingual environments. We use the word *radical* intentionally; one of the first conversations we have with prospective Language Explorer teachers invites them to first define and describe the culture of schooling as it is now, and then participate in a visioning process in which they reimagine school as affirming and culturally robust. What would school look like? Feel like? Sound like? As our work together evolves, we invite educators to discard those policies and pedagogical practices that silence, marginalize, or otherwise confine students' humanity, and instead create classroom communities that authentically reflect the personal, cultural, and linguistic identities and values of their participants.

Within the context of the SLA, educators model this interruption by developing classroom routines that reflect students' requests/inquiries for food, space, sound, silence, and breaks; using their own identity and experience to model key projects (e.g., by creating and sharing verbal and artistic renderings of their own multiple identities before asking students to do the same); and positioning students' languages, families, cultural traditions, and artwork as authoritative "texts." Throughout, students work collaboratively to define, customize, and complete final projects, determine how to share their work with other classes and their families, and make recommendations to improve teaching and learning during the academic year. Thus, the SLA engages students as key stakeholders within the classroom and community at large, while simultaneously challenging educators to unlearn and reconstruct their approach to teaching, learning, and culturally responsive classroom leadership (Fraise & Brooks, 2015).

This can be a stretch for some teachers, many of whom are deeply socialized into schooling-as-usual. Over the past 2 decades, there has been an explosion of neoliberal policies in teacher preparation and K–12 schooling alike; as we note in Chapter 1, these often frame teaching as a technical, rather than a professional, endeavor. In our role as teacher educators, for example, we have witnessed the impact of high-stakes teacher performance assessments (TPAs), a form of standardized evaluation that emphasizes task fidelity and precise compliance with technical directions over the use of authentic, contextually responsive practice (Dover, 2018; Kleyn, López, & Makar, 2015). Despite advocates' claims that TPAs can be used within the context of culturally responsive practice (e.g., Lynn, 2014), research demonstrates that they dramatically disrupt teacher candidates' development of their self-efficacy, autonomy, and agency (Dover, 2018) and effectively dislocate, sterilize, and "whitewash" teacher preparation overall (Au, 2013; Henning, Dover, Dotson, & Agarwal-Rangnath, 2018; Madeloni & Gorlewski, 2013; Tuck & Gorlewski, 2016).

In our own work with teachers of newcomer and emergent plurilingual students, we seek not to "train" teachers in a specific set of culturally and linguistically responsive practices, but rather to nourish their development of the professional expertise and agency necessary to teach in radically inclusive ways. Thus, unlike didactic models of professional development, which too often replicate banking-model processes (where trainers "deposit" knowledge into teachers) while instructing educators to be Freiran problem-posers (1970/2000) in their own classrooms, our professional learning sessions center teachers' examination of the experiences, beliefs, and practices that shape their approach to teaching and learning. As teachers explore their own assumptions, socialization, and values, we embed opportunities to consider and experiment with new curricular, pedagogical, and structural approaches.

EXPERIENTIAL PEDAGOGY AS PROFESSIONAL LEARNING

Thus, in addition to training related to translanguaging pedagogy, we also focus professional learning on co-teaching, co-planning, and inquiry-oriented teaching. Throughout, we emphasize strategies for creating "humanizing classrooms" (Paris & Alim, 2017) and engage faculty in team-building activities, including the creation and sharing of poetry, narrative, and art. One of our core values within the Language Explorer program is that we never ask students to do *anything* we have not already done ourselves and, given the types of artistic and literary activities woven throughout the curriculum, this means that faculty take a lot of personal and professional risks. In their first hours together, instructional teams will discuss their multiple social identities, linguistic fluencies, and experiences with privilege and marginalization. They will write and read poetry, create and share self-portraits, and practice reading and making meaning of literature written in a language they do not speak (see the companion website for examples of some of these professional learning activities).

For many educators, the idea of bringing our "whole selves" to the classroom is both unfamiliar and precious. We strive to model this throughout professional learning, as we share our own experiences with linguistic oppression (as was the case for Ferran, who was forced to silence his native language of Catalán throughout his K–12 schooling in Spain), growth, and monolingualism (in the case of Alison, who grew up monolingual and monocultural, and is working toward biliteracy). We model our co-planning process, focusing on how we reconcile different ideas about curriculum or pedagogy, use our own poetry as examples for annotation, and share artwork we created with our children and families (see Figures 3.1 and 3.2).

Unsurprisingly, some teachers struggle with or resist the idea of writing poetry or creating art; "but I can't draw" is a common complaint, to which we invariably reply with some version of "neither can we!" Nevertheless, we stretch, just as we require our students to stretch. Throughout, we remind teachers of Freire's (2005) challenge to avoid the "hypocrisy of [being] one who while saying it does opposite" (p. 98). We are not professional

Figure 3.1. Teacher Juan Pablo García Shares His Language Journey

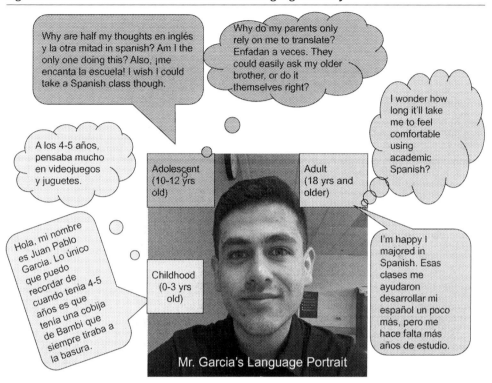

In this "language selfie," teacher Juan Pablo García models how he reflects about his languaging at different points in his life.

poets, artists, or performers. However, by braving up and becoming vulnerable in the classroom, we all have the opportunity to nourish educational spaces that invite, affirm, and sustain the humanity of all participants.

FORMING, STORMING, NORMING, AND PERFORMING: FROM TEACHER TO TEAM

In describing how groups function, Tuckman (1965) identified four key stages in group performance: forming, norming, storming, and performing. At each phase of development, groups have different needs and different struggles. During the forming stage, groups are getting to know one another and their task; during this period, they require significant guidance from facilitators in order to define their work and move successfully through the "storming" phase (as initial conflicts arise). If successfully coached through emergent tensions, groups enter into norming and performing stages,

Figure 3.2. Language Explorer Teacher Heriberto Olive's autobiographical comic

Figures 3.1 and 3.2 are examples of models used during professional learning sessions for teachers.

where they learn to function independently and efficiently, drawing on the strengths of each member.

We see similar trends within our work with teachers. Our early professional learning workshops are designed to help teachers get to know one another as people, educators, and collaborators so that they can work effectively throughout the Language Explorer program. For many, Language Explorers offers an unprecedented opportunity to work with and learn from colleagues who share their vision and values, and the teams come together quickly. For others, however, braving up will mean making dramatic shifts in how they understand authority and autonomy in the classroom . . . and that can be a "stormy" experience.

When building instructional teams, we strategically build teams that are diverse in culture, discipline, years of experience, and approach to teaching literature and language. It is not uncommon for an instructional team to consist of, for example, a monolingual preservice art teacher, a veteran instructional assistant who speaks English and Portuguese, and a third-year science teacher who speaks English and Spanish; another team might include a preservice math teacher who speaks English and Vietnamese, a first-year instructional assistant who speaks English and Spanish, and a monolingual veteran English language arts teacher. Overall, our goal is to balance teachers' unique strengths and epistemological orientations as well as ensure each team is a) multilingual and b) includes a teacher who is an "emergent bilingual" in need of scaffolding. Assuming we are successful in our coaching, teams' cultural, linguistic, and epistemological diversity should prepare them to model collaboration, pedagogical creativity, and linguistic fluidity in their work with students. In the past, for example, language arts teachers have taken leadership in building activities related to connotation and detonation in poetry (see Chapter 5); math teachers have adapted personal timeline activities into scaled graphs of relative influence (see Chapter 5); and science teachers have coached their peers in applying scientific concepts (such as ecological models of community) to analyses of identity or literature (see Chapter 4).

Karina is a preservice Spanish teacher who worked with the SLA during the year before and after her yearlong student teaching placement. In reflecting on the ways teaching in the Language Explorer programs was different from what she experienced at other school sites, she highlighted the mindfulness and curiosity that characterized her team's collaboration, using the metaphor of a "ladder" to describe the way her team members supported one another and their students:

> [We are] three separate identities coming together. As two legs and a rung that support each other to build towards climbing higher and higher. Since we are

able to work together, we then provide strength and support to our students to climb to their next level and beyond. As a team, we have established the respect of actively listening to each other's ideas and making sure that we equally have a role in the classroom.

Karina's appreciation for the interconnected nature of her team's work is a common theme among Language Explorer faculty, many of whom attest to the ways their initial vulnerability nourished effective and efficient collaborations in the classroom.

However, no partnership is perfect, and we frequently see "storming" as teams struggle against their own professional socialization or come up against professional or cultural differences. This can create dissonance within teams, especially for teachers whose daily work conditions are in contradiction with the collaborative, emergent curricular and pedagogical processes valued within the Language Explorers. One of our faculty, Guillermo (a veteran Spanish teacher), for example, struggled to share authority with colleagues he considered "less qualified," including the preservice teachers and instructional assistants with whom he was partnered. In reflecting on the efficacy of his teaching team, he commented that

> Diffusing responsibilities among three adults in a classroom has its pros and cons. Who takes the lead? What if two people disagree as to content, delivery, or student activities? . . . Also, what is the role of an intern? Instructional Assistant? Credentialed Teacher? Are the intern and credentialed teacher equals? I feel that having all students view the adults as "teachers" is important, but it's an important opportunity for interns to understand that they are not experienced, credentialed teachers.

Thus, in order to brave up, Guillermo had to find ways to interrupt the patterns of socialization that undermine our individual and collective capacity to learn from and draw on the cultural, linguistic, and experiential wisdom of our colleagues and students.

Ironically, while Guillermo was grappling with his own resistance to sharing instructional authority, one of his co-teachers, Monique, was building relationships with students and visiting other classrooms to observe their instructional approach. Monique, who at the time was a preservice teacher of mathematics, was the only teacher at her school site who was fluent in Turkish, as well as a recent immigrant herself. She spoke regularly of her own journey and attempts to acclimate to U.S. society; this led some students, and especially non-Spanish-speaking students, to identify more with Monique than with her colleagues. Throughout the summer, students approached Monique to tell their stories of migration, and occasionally of trauma, and she became a sitewide conduit for empathy and community resources. Thus, despite Guillermo's frustration with having to share authority with someone he considered "less qualified," Monique was actually a significant asset within the program. In reflecting on her experience as a Language Explorer teacher, Monique described it as "wonderful," in that

> . . . it allowed students to open up and share, instead of being shy and embarrassed about their English not being "perfect." I feel like they felt understood, empathized with and had a sense of belonging. I wish we could have gone on for all of summer. I am sure we would see the same enthusiasm in attendance till the very last day . . .
>
> I [also] learned so much. First of all, the team had so many amazing ideas. I was constantly taking pictures of different activities in my class and other classes. I learned although teenagers are a big group that is written off as disrespectful and mean, they necessarily are not . . . I realized that although I am twice their age, I shared so much with them, when it comes to music, being new to the U.S., family issues, etc. I feel like this program helped me grow not only as a teacher but also as a mom and a human.

As program directors, part of our work is helping teams of teachers work through the storming phase of development and reimagine what it means to collaborate—with one another and with their students—so they can fully benefit from the strengths, perspectives, and resources present in the classroom. Thus, rather than seeing the tensions of collaboration as "failures," we recast them as productive disruptions that offer opportunities to develop the personal, professional, and communicative skills necessary to bring collaborative, student-driven, and transformative teaching back to their school sites.

In the following chapters, we explore the types of curricular and pedagogical experiences that characterize our work with newcomer and emergent plurilingual students and communities. Throughout, we feature examples of student work and teachers' efforts to learn with, from, and about their students. In so doing, we wish to underscore that we seek to nourish educational spaces where we not only celebrate diversity, but where we interrogate, affirm, amplify, and are accountable to it. In so doing, we echo the words of Alim and Paris (2017), whose scholarship regarding culturally sustaining pedagogy reminds us that

> . . . a critical centering of the valued ways of youth and communities of color in education is a radical act, an act made possible by the work of many in our collective and across the centuries of struggle in our communities, an act that disrupts a schooling system centered on ideologies of White, middle-class,

monolingual, cisheteropatriarchal, able-bodies superiority . . . CSP [culturally sustaining pedagogy], like all critical asset-based approaches, is at heart about survival—a survival we want to sustain through education—and about changing the conditions under which we live and work by opening up new and revitalizing community rooted ways of thinking about education beyond, as Morrison reminded us, "the White gaze," . . . where children of color can both survive and thrive. (p. 12)

In the pages that follow, we invite you to join students and teachers from the Language Explorers in braving up and finding new ways to co-create "education beyond," where we all have the voice, confidence, and agency to speak up and out for the education our communities deserve.

Resources and Reflective Activities for Chapter 3

- In this chapter, we suggest reconceptualizing classrooms as global villages. What identities, languages, and cultures are currently visible in your classroom? How can you build a space where the stories and linguistic repertoires of all students are amplified and interconnected? What would you have to shift about your stance, design, or pedagogy to strategically and intentionally co-construct a plurilingual classroom discourse?
- In Figures 3.1 and 3.2, we provide examples of how educators can share their own journeys as they model vulnerability, metacognition about languaging, and linguistic experimentation. What parts of your story do you currently share with your students and colleagues? What aspects of yourself do you hide or silence? Why?
- Braving up requires experimentation. Create an artifact that you could use to share your story with students and discuss it with a colleague. Why did you decide on this specific artifact? How did you stretch while creating it?

If I Were to Change the World, by Gea Lopez

If I were to change the world,
I'd cancel discrimination,
I'd cancel division between cultures
I'd even cancel hate to people, cultures, languages.

If I were in charge of the world,
Tendrian que dejar de criticar a la gente por la religión
en la que creen,
There would be respect to everyone,
There would even be world peace,

If I were in charge of the world
No serias dicriminado, por tu acento o por tu color de
piel
No serias aislado de la gente
No tendrias que cambiar solo para encajar en algúin
lugar.

If I were in charge of the world . . .
No habria mas odio,
Solo por que simplemente no te gusta lo que la
sociedad dice o como "siempre se a hecho"

And a person who doesn't discriminate its always a
better person
And sometimes love makes everything better
Would still be allowed to have our opinion but never
hurt people
In charge of the world

by Gea Lopez

Part II

RADICALLY INCLUSIVE PEDAGOGIES

CHAPTER 4

Who Are You? Exploring Identity and Community in the Classroom

Far too many language learners sit silent and unknown in classrooms, wondering if anyone knows or cares what they are thinking, wish to say, or have to contribute. Meanwhile, their often well-meaning teachers look out at the faces before them and see not individuals brimming with stories and questions, but a sea of labels describing students' linguistic deficits. As part of braving up, educators have to disrupt the cycle of centering what emergent plurilingual students "have not" rather than recognizing, embracing, and valuing who they *are*. Thus, in our Language Explorer classrooms, teachers begin by using the question "Who are you?" as a pathway toward creating relevant, culturally and linguistically sustaining, and academically rigorous classrooms. When educators take the time to get to know our students as individual students, members of the academic community, and cultural and linguistic beings, we have opportunities to see and affirm each student's unique linguistic register, variances, and richness. We can then build classrooms that amplify, leverage, and expand our collective linguistic repertoires and norms of academic discourse. In so doing, classrooms become spaces not of linguistic exclusion but linguistic experimentation, as teachers and students brave up and raise their dynamic voices.

In this chapter, we focus on strategies for inviting students to explore and share their multicultural and plurilingual identities as a means of building classroom community, fostering engagement, nourishing student voice, and bridging to subject area content. We explore ways to deepen teachers' and students' conceptual understanding of and linguistic repertoires for discussing identity, using examples of student-created poetry, art, and narrative writing to illustrate how activities might unfold.

BREAKING THE SILENCE

As described in Chapter 3, one of the most notable features of the first day of our Language Explorer programs is silence. Despite teachers' best efforts to create welcoming spaces—their enthusiastic welcome of students, their multilingual playlist of contemporary music, the artwork adorning the walls—it is always the same: students enter the room silently, unsure of whether anyone else in the room will speak their language, afraid to raise their voice lest they do it "wrong."

In other educational settings, this silence is treated as the "normal" response for students who have been stigmatized with deficit labels such as Limited English Proficiency, English Language Learner, or Standard English Language Learner (Flores & Rosa, 2019). For decades, silence has been associated with students' focus, learning, or signal of respect and reflective thinking (Caranfa, 2006). In other contexts, silence can indicate disinterest, disengagement, or resistance, as students shut down in response to—or as protection against—irrelevant, culturally insensitive, linguistically inaccessible, or overtly oppressive curriculum, pedagogy, or policy (e.g., Kohl, 1995).

As part of pre-program professional learning sessions, our Language Explorer teachers prepare to model plurilingualism, affirm linguistic experimentation, and position themselves as co-learners from the moment students enter the classroom. In addition to interrogating their own languaging practices (by, for example, noting how often they speak in the classroom, and in which languages), they also (a) plan multimedia, multilingual introductions of themselves; (b) select classroom artifacts that represent the cultural, geographic, and linguistic diversity of the instructional team; and (c) prepare to describe key concepts in plurilingual and visual ways. Our goal is for students to immediately feel the difference between normative (monoglossic) educational settings and the Language Explorer classroom, so they begin to consciously (and unconsciously) reframe the "problem" in the classroom as not their own multidimensional linguistic repertoires, but the systems that silence them.

However, all of the preparation in the world does little to alter the dynamics of the first day. Students enter our Language Explorer classrooms with preexisting experiences of linguistic oppression and little reason to trust educators they do not yet know. Thus, teachers strive to consciously interpret students' silence not as their own failure or a sign of students' disinterest, but as opportunity, as anticipation, as the precious moments during which students are deciding whether it is safe to voice their thoughts, ideas, and wishes. As teachers brave up, they learn to notice moments of silence, embrace it with respect (if not with comfort!), and begin to use it as a launchpad. Thus, rather than jumping right into content, our Language Explorer teachers focus their first interactions with students on formally inviting students' multicultural selves and plurilingual voices into the classroom and on challenging the institutional structures that position students as passive "objects" of educational spaces (Freire, 1970/2000).

NOURISHING BRAVE, HETEROGLOSSIC CLASSROOMS

Educators have long advocated for the importance of "safe spaces" where students feel comfortable in the classroom and can speak their mind without fear of judgment. In recent years, however, the concept of classrooms as "safe spaces" has been challenged. This reflects the reality that classrooms have historically been anything but safe for students of color, plurilingual students, LGBTQ+ students, and students from other historically minoritized groups, and acknowledges that it takes bravery to confront normative paradigms that perpetuate injustice. In the words of Boostrom (1998), "learning necessarily involves not merely risk, but the pain of giving up a former condition in favour of a new way of seeing things" (p. 399). Arao and Clemens (2013) encourage educators to avoid seeking safety by setting simplistic ground rules (such as "agree to disagree" and "don't take things personally") that whitewash pluralism and avoid engaging complexities. Instead, they challenge teachers to nourish "brave spaces" in which they work collaboratively with students to establish new, liberatory classroom norms, where students have the scaffolding to directly engage complex and controversial ideas, opportunities to develop individual and collective accountability, and the support to challenge their own and others' assumptions.

Within the context of the Language Explorers, creating a brave space requires teachers to adopt what we call an *inclusive understanding of language*, or IUL, in which teachers acknowledge and explore the multilayered and complex interrelationships among students' cultural and linguistic identities and experiences. When adopting this lens, teachers engage students' funds of language (a construct that reflects an extension of Moll, Amanti, Neff, & Gonzalez's [1992] emphasis on students' cultural "funds of knowledge" as assets they bring to the classroom), raciolinguistic identities (including both the ways students define their own racial and linguistic identities, and how those identities are ascribed to students without their knowledge or consent), existing and emergent critical consciousness (overall, and their metalinguistic consciousness specifically), and daily languaging practices. In so doing, teachers disrupt normative monoglossic ideologies and instead nourish heteroglossic classrooms in which each students' unique linguistic repertoire is framed as an essential asset (our

Language Explorer teachers often refer to students as having "plurilingual superpowers") that only they can contribute to a linguistic multitude that "can never be flattened into sameness, unity, identity, or indifference" (Negri & Hardt, 2005, p. 105).

BRAVING UP BY SHARING WHO YOU ARE

Unlike banking models of education (Freire, 1970/2000), in which teachers hold all the power and attempt to "deposit" knowledge into their students, braving up requires teachers to explicitly and implicitly engage students as co-creators of and co-investigators within a pluralistic educational community. By necessity, this requires us to not just adopt a series of strategies or tools, but to fundamentally shift the way we think about teaching and learning. As part of this transformation, all of our Language Explorer programs are grounded within three core principles: modeling, open dialogues, and co-learning.

Principle One: We Do Every Project First

Research attests to the importance of modeling in the classroom, with abundant examples of its impact on students' development of literacy and general academic skills. Much of this work is grounded in Pearson and Gallagher's (1983) "gradual release of responsibility" model, in which teachers slowly and strategically move from teacher-regulated to student-regulated learning, providing cognitive and academic scaffolding to support students' independence (e.g., Buehl, 2014; Fisher & Frey, 2013; Wilhelm, Baker, & Dube, 2001). This "I do, we do, you do" approach is far from new to our Language Explorer teachers; most regularly use modeling in their academic year classrooms.

However, unlike normative classrooms, where modeling is often focused on concrete academic skills, such as "active reading" or approaches to problem solving, Language Explorer teachers use modeling as a form of academic disruption; our teachers use themselves as models to illustrate principles of vulnerability, humanity, and linguistic experimentation. In the Language Explorer program, teachers do *every single project* themselves before assigning work to students. This practice, which we consider a nonnegotiable element of the Language Explorers, enables teachers to reflect on their academic and linguistic processes, share diverse examples of draft and final work (as no two teachers within an instructional team will create identical work), and situate themselves as co-learners within the classroom community.

Examples of teacher-created projects are visible throughout this book, from science teacher Heriberto Olive's autobiographical comic (Figure 3.2), to preservice teacher Sabino Reyes's personal timeline (Figure 5.3), to the community ecosystem created by art teacher Shawna Dinnen (Figure 4.1). In this illustration, Shawna adapted Bronfenbrenner's (1977) ecological model of human development to illustrate her own situated identities within her multiple communities. The innermost circle depicts her immediate personal relationships (her "microsystem"); the next, her identity as a member of her geographic and cultural community (her "mesosystem");

Figure 4.1. Exploring Our Community's Ecology

Community ecosystem created by Language Explorer teacher Shawna Dinnen.

and the outermost circle her identity within a broader global and sociopolitical world (her "exosystem").

For Shawna, an art teacher who, at the time, identified as monolingual in English, using her artistic skills to model identity exploration provided an invaluable opportunity to both model vulnerability and encourage students to experiment with new ways of representing their own cultural and linguistic selves. In her words,

> Before/during the introduction of the "bullseye" Multiple Communities project, I made the project more personal for the students by posing ideas and introducing them to what MY multiple communities are. My reasoning for doing this was to push students to dive deeper into their own understanding of what community is, other than where they live and their neighbors. We discussed different ideas of community while referencing my community poster, the images of the special people, food and places that create my multiple communities and if I could not translate what I was saying in English into Spanish or Russian I would act it out. Giving them my definition of community verbally, visually, translating some examples and using exaggerated body language to communicate really helped [me share myself and] the students to expand their ideas of what their community really is.

Figure 4.2 illustrates how students built upon Shawna's example when creating their own community ecosystems.

In the days that followed, Shawna and her co-teachers used this project as a springboard for deeper explorations of students' personal and social identities, analyses of the layers of community experienced by literary characters, and activities where students practiced active literacy skills as they asked and answered questions about their identities, experiences, and communities.

Principle Two: Open Dialogue

Unlike monoglossic classroom spaces, where dialogue is frequently unidirectional and hyperregulated, our Language Explorer classrooms are grounded in principles of authentic open dialogue. When braving up, teachers don't position themselves as all-knowing "masters" of the classroom, but rather look for creative ways to demonstrate and model interpersonal and linguistic curiosity. From their first days in the classroom, educators strive to talk with—not to—students as they investigate shared questions, co-construct meaning, and decide on the parameters of activities. Throughout, teachers listen closely to learn from the unique ways newcomer and emergent plurilingual students experience their own identities, leverage their linguistic

Figure 4.2. Student-Created Examples of Their Community Ecosystems

repertoires, and reconstruct "school" as an affirming, plurilingual, and collaboratively built space.

In the classroom, educators model this principle of open dialogue by working toward transparency about instructional processes (for example, by openly discussing why they do what they do in the classroom), as well as by sharing their own personal, professional, and linguistic vulnerabilities. These might include educators' own experiences as emergent plurilinguals (who are learning to use language in new ways), open discussions of how and why co-teachers approached a specific project differently, or explorations of how various aspects of teachers' identities manifest—or are hidden—within specific professional contexts.

Within the Language Explorers, we frame this as not only "dialoguing and participating," but also as an act of critical consciousness; our students' experiences and voices do not emerge in a vacuum—instead, their experiences are shaped by their broader sociopolitical and sociolinguistic experiences (see Rodríguez, Monreal, & Howard, 2020). As we authentically listen to and learn from newcomer and emergent plurilingual students, educators have both the opportunity and the responsibility to work toward liberation.

Principle Three: We Are All Teachers and Learners

In describing his philosophy, South African activist Desmond Tutu referred to the concept of *Ubuntu*, a Nguni word often translated as "I am, because you are." In Tutu's words,

> My humanity is caught up, is inextricably bound up, in yours. We belong in a bundle of life. We say a person is a person through other persons. It is not I think therefore I am. It says rather: I am human because I belong, I participate, and I share. A person with Ubuntu is open and available to others, affirming of others, does not feel threatened that others are able and good, for he or she has a proper self-assurance that comes from knowing that he or she belongs in a greater whole and is diminished when others are humiliated or diminished, when others are tortured or oppressed, or treated as if they were less than who they are. (Desmond Tutu Peace Foundation, 2017, n.p.)

Ubuntu underscores the idea that all people are interconnected, and thus the stories we tell aren't our individual stories but collective stories that are shaped not only by the individual telling them, but by the collective created among the teller(s), the listener(s), and every member of the community who participated in creating this moment.

This concept of co-creation and shared storytelling is visible throughout the Language Explorer curriculum and pedagogy. It also shapes our approach to staffing and supporting instructional teams, through our unique approach to educational hierarchy. Unlike normative classrooms, where a single (English-speaking) educator holds all of the instructional and linguistic power, with students and additional adults (such as paraprofessionals or instructional aides) positioned as objects, subjects, or supports within the classroom, we construct teaching and learning as co-created and shared endeavors. For example, although our instructional teams are comprised of educators who typically have very different roles (veteran teacher, instructional assistant, and preservice teacher) and varying linguistic fluencies, within the context of the Language Explorers, each educator is explicitly positioned as a "lead teacher" who initiates, expands, and sustains class-room interactions. This practice both models the disruption of normative, monoglossic processes, and ensures that each classroom team is able to leverage the unique perspectives, cultural and professional expertise, and linguistic repertoires of its members.

When introducing this model to prospective teachers, we focus on the following three levels of collegiality:

- Level 1—Collegiality within each instructional team: All members of the instructional team introduce themselves as "teachers" and are expected to candidly share their linguistic expertise and learning edges. All educators have the same responsibilities when planning and teaching.
- Level 2—Collegiality between teams/classrooms: In normative educational practice, teachers often function as silos, with little opportunity for shared imagination. By contrast, our Language Explorer programs include time for daily collective planning and debriefing. At the end of each instructional day, teams come together to share how they adapted, modified, and enhanced the curriculum. This dialogue truly fosters a comprehensive program spirit by promoting active listening and learning across all teams.
- Level 3—Collegiality between teachers and students: In the Language Explorer programs, teachers brave up by sharing their own identities, vulnerabilities, and experiences with students. In so doing, they disrupt the typical hierarchies of the classroom and model the principle of interconnectedness.

Collectively, these three principles establish a foundation for building classrooms as shared, heteroglossic spaces in which educators and students can bravely embark on a collaborative educational and linguistic journey. In the pages that follow, we examine how teachers and students begin this journey, offering examples of ways educators can elicit, engage, and affirm plurilingual students' identities, experiences, and stories from their first moment in the classroom.

INVITING STUDENTS IN

Science teacher Juan Pablo García first joined the Language Explorer com-munity as a preservice teacher, when he was invited to be part of the in-structional team at one of our partner districts. Like many teachers, Juan describes his experience with the Language Explorers as both personally and professional transformative; Juan's own parents were forced to work in the fields rather than attend school. Juan draws upon his family's experiences when approaching his own work as a teacher, and at the time of publication—just 2 years after earning his teaching credential—Juan serves as his school's instructional lead for dual-language science and a mentor to incoming Language Explorer educators. In describing his approach to teaching emergent plurilingual students, Juan begins by asking himself, "What can I do to invite students into the unknown world of [the classroom]?"

> I try to think of activities where the students can pull from something they feel confident enough to share regardless of the language they decide to participate in. For example: sharing their favorite artist, favorite food or favorite video game. I also make sure to place myself as a participant in the activity rather than the leader or the one in control. I want to both show and model how to be vulnerable in the classroom, something I don't expect to see within the first few days we are together. I know that many of the activities will still be received with silence but I know that with time students will slowly warm up to me and one another.

In order to meet this goal of inviting students into the world of the unknown, Language Explorer teachers use a series of activities, or scaffolds, to support students in seeing themselves as necessary and valued members of a heteroglossic whole.

EXPLORING IDENTITY: WHO ARE YOU?

In each of our Language Explorer classrooms, we begin by challenging students to answer the question, "Who are you?" While their initial responses typically center surface-level depictions of their identities (the color of their hair, the hobbies they enjoy), as they build confidence and *confianza* (trust in the *reciprocidad*/reciprocity of relationships), they begin to share deeper and more meaningful aspects of their identities. Educators then provide linguistic and social scaffolds to support students in experimenting with how to use language as a liberatory tool, through which they read—and speak—their world with critical eyes (Davis, 2018; Sonu & Aguilar, 2017).

Like many of our Language Explorers, Ashley[6] entered our classroom poised for silence. Would she be seen? Would she be heard? Would her humanity be cherished and affirmed, or would she be pushed to the margins? As her teachers invited her into the unknown, she began to reveal the swirling thoughts behind her silence, ultimately creating the poem shown as

Figure 4.3. See Chapter 3, and the companion website at www.bravingup .com, for additional resources related to teaching and modeling autobiographical poetry, and see Chapter 7 for examples of students' plurilingual poetry.

In addition to demonstrating Ashley's grappling with her identities—and how they manifest within and are mediated by oppressive educational spaces—this poem shows the increasing syntactic and linguistic complexity that emerges within Language Explorer classrooms. In just a few short lines, Ashley demonstrates how newcomer and emergent plurilingual students negotiate and navigate their own silences, uncertainties, and intersectionality. She effectively frames her experiences of dissonance (wondering, but being unable to find answers; hearing music but not understanding its context; pretending in order to accept reality), strategically uses contractions to emphasize meaning (e.g., through the use of "can't" and "don't" in lines 1, 4, and 6, but "do not" in 11), and implicitly challenges readers to do better (so she can do more than pretend to give her best). Moreover, as is the case for many newcomer and emergent plurilingual students (Rodríguez, Monreal, & Howard, 2020), Ashley's poem underscores the complexities she is forced to navigate as a minoritized, immigrant student of color.

Within the context of compulsory education, students rarely shift from silence to poetry organically; instead, poems like Ashley's emerge in response to educators' persistent and strategic efforts to nourish brave, affirming, and heteroglossic classrooms. In the pages that follow, we explore

Figure 4.3. I Am Ashley

I Am Ashley

I am Ashley, I don't know who I am.
I wonder sometimes what was the origin
Of humanity and everything that exists
But . . . I can't find the answer.
I hear music most of the time
Because I don't understand the world.
I see the mirror every day and
I ask myself . . . Who am I?
Why am I here?
I want to return to Mexico with my family.
I am Ashley, I do not know who I am
I pretend to give the best of myself
And accept reality

---

some of the activities teachers can use to invite students into the unknown, scaffold student inquiry, and support students in finding ways to use their agency to co-create schools in which they no longer have to pretend.

Scaffold 1: Name Tags

Research attests to the importance of students feeling known in the classroom, and the trauma that occurs when educators fail to learn, mispronounce, or alter students' names (Kohli & Solórzano, 2012). As part of our effort to welcome students' identities, individualities, and pluralities, Language Explorer teachers begin each new class by inviting students to create trifold name tags through which they share their names and some of the visible and invisible characteristics that make them unique (see the companion website at www.bravingup.com for examples and templates). Students then share their names and identities in small groups, practice pronouncing one another's names (which, given the cultural linguistic diversity of Language Explorer classrooms, often requires repeated efforts), and begin to identify ways in which they are similar to and unique among their classmates. Through this process, educators support students in moving from superficial analyses of their physical appearance or likes and dislikes toward deeper analyses of the characteristics that remain beneath the surface, such as the traits that define their personality, their values, and the complexities of their sociolinguistic and geopolitical identities.

Within the Language Explorer program, we emphasize that language and identity are not static truths, but dynamic and ever-changing iterations. Thus, as students continue to reflect upon, unpack, and unfold their multiple layers of experiences, they will continue to add to and revise their name tags, incorporating new images, plurilingual references, and "secret selves" (sometimes written in invisible ink, in order to underscore their privacy; see Chapter 5 for more on the use of invisible ink in Language Explorer classrooms).

Scaffold 2: Visual Representations of Community

As part of their effort to nourish heteroglossic, pluralistic classroom spaces, Language Explorer teachers work strategically not only to invite students' identities and humanity into the classroom, but also to explicitly position school as not a space into which students must assimilate, but instead as one that is created by—and cannot exist without—the unique contributions of each student. Ideologically, we frame this through the lens of humanizing and decolonizing educational practice (Bartolomé; 1994; Freire, 1970/2000; Salazar, 2013; Valenzuela, 1999), in which educators both deeply care for their students and also prepare them to question the status quo of schooling and the monoglossic and standardized ideologies that shape it. In the words of Sintos Coloma (2020), teachers must understand "*el sitio/* the place" where they are teaching and learning from language learners as well as "*la lengua/*the language" used in the teaching and learning practices implemented in the classroom. This act of conscientization about *el sitio y la lengua* can prepare educators to disrupt the norms that silence and minoritize plurilingual students, and support students in coming to believe they—and their languaging, and their perspectives, and their humanity—truly *belong* in the classroom.

Over the years, we have used many strategies and metaphors to visually illustrate these principles of heteroglossia and pluralism. These have included the creation of community puzzles, in which each student and educator created a multimedia puzzle piece representing their unique contribution to the classroom whole (Figure 4.4), to communal murals (Figure 4.5), to a metaphorical forest of life in which each student created a cultural and linguistic tree to plant in our common forest (Figure 4.6; see also Chapter 8).

In each case, we rely on the principles described earlier in this chapter in that teachers begin by creating and sharing their own diverse, plurilingual examples, and then model active listening and co-learning as students share, analyze, and ask questions about one another's contributions. See the companion website at www.bravingup.com for templates and instructional resources related to each of these visual representations of community; Chapter 7 also features strategies for use in online and virtual classrooms.

Scaffold 3: Micrography

The previous examples are relatively low-risk for our Language Explorer students in that students can create and curate contributions nonverbally (for example, by choosing to collage images rather than describe their identities in words) or making public or private decisions about how to represent their linguistic repertoire. By contrast, micrography is a scaffold that supports students in bridging from visual representations of identity to linguistic ones; in so doing, it functions as both an informal assessment of the scope of students' linguistic repertoire and an opportunity for educators to begin explicitly stretching the linguistic boundaries of the classroom.

Micrography is a form of art in which artists use words to create line drawings. In the Language Explorer classroom, we begin by taking and printing high-contrast photographs of students; students then trace the contours of their images in pencil, and then add words to fill in their

Figure 4.4. Student-Created Community Puzzle

After creating individual puzzle pieces, students build a shared community puzzle; they then analyze it for common themes, symbols, and emphases.

Figure 4.5. Student-Created Class Mural

After examining symbolism in literature, students chose a symbol to represent a hidden aspect of their identity. This mural depicts who students are "beneath the surface."

features (eyes, hair, lips) with nouns, adjectives, adverbs, and verbs that define their identities. As students consider the concrete aspects of their identity (nouns), their nuances and future possibilities (adjectives), the ways they move and flow within their worlds (adverbs), and themselves as active beings (verbs), they create a linguistic self-portrait. Considered as a collective, students' self-portraits create a syntactic symphony in which each word and its linguistic functionality illustrates the plurilingual melodies and rhythms of the classroom. See Figure 4.7 for examples of student micrographies; additional resources can be found at www.bravingup.com and at Teachers College Press at tcpress.com/dover-resources.

In addition to being a fun and accessible way to interweave image, identity, and languaging, micrographies are also tools to support students in developing their visual literacies. In micrography, words are not just

Figure 4.6. A Student Presenting Her Tree of Life

After learning about deep, surface, and shallow manifestations of culture, students create a community forest composed of trees depicting each student's unique roots and blossoms.

Figure 4.7. Student-Created Micrographies

words; they must be considered through the lens of languaging and positionality. Placing the word *trust* near one's brain, for example, might have a different meaning than placing the same word near the heart or lips; this analysis of positionality supports students' evolving knowledge of semantics, or how the meanings of words change based on their context. Similarly, as students make decisions about which named languages to represent in their portraits—and how—they begin to think strategically about the multiple functions of their unique linguistic repertoire.

When educators support and challenge students to brave up, expand their zones of cultural comfort (Rodríguez-Valls, 2009), and co-create affirming, heteroglossic classroom spaces, we begin to act as co-conspirators who can embolden students in their fight to voice their personas and reclaim classrooms—and academic discourse—as belonging to the plurilingual, transcultural majority. In the coming chapters, we examine ways educators can guide students in shifting from explorations of their personal identities into an analysis of our shared social identities, a process Language Explorer educator Zineh Abu Khalaf describes as "moving from thinking about who you are as an I to exploring who we are as a We."

Resources and Reflective Activities for Chapter 4

- In this chapter, we explore some of the ways teachers can use arts-based pedagogy to support community-building and linguistic experimentation. Create your own name tag or community puzzle piece, using or adapting one of the templates on our companion website. Share your work with a colleague, and discuss the words, symbols, and images you each chose to include. What can you learn from looking at similarities and differences in the way you approached this activity?

- The companion website includes instructional resources and video tutorials related to micrography. Use these to create your own micrographic self-portrait, and discuss your work with a friend or colleague. What was easy or hard about this activity? How did you select the words and languages you featured in your self-portrait? How did you decide on the placement of individual words?

- The companion website includes additional resources related to learning students' names, exploring surface and deep culture, and creating community forests. To access these and other resources, visit www .bravingup.com or Teachers College Press at tcpress.com/dover-resources.

CHAPTER 5

Who Are We? Crossing Borders With Arts-Based and Plurilingual Pedagogies

EMBRACING OUR BORDERLANDS

In 2006, Alison was a Language Arts teacher in a predominantly Puerto Rican school district in Massachusetts. At the time, Massachusetts was one of many states subject to a monoglossic, "English-only" mandate, which required that *"children learn to read and write solely in English"* (Commonwealth of Massachusetts, 2002). Thus, while monolingual, English-speaking students were required to take "foreign language" courses, emergent plurilingual students were denied the opportunity to leverage their full linguistic repertoire; teachers could use only "a minimal amount of the child's native language when necessary" for a period of no more than 1 year, exclusively within the context of English Language Development classes, provided "no subject matter [is] taught in any language other than English." Unsurprisingly, policies like this have a dramatic and destructive impact on newcomer and plurilingual students; few of Alison's colleagues spoke—or saw a reason to learn—Spanish, and just 29% of the district's Latinx students, and 8% of students designated as "current or former English Learners," scored at or above proficiency on the state mandated 10th-grade English Language Arts standardized test (Massachusetts Department of Education, 2007).

As we discussed in Chapter 2, deficit bilingualism is an ideology through which emergent plurilingual students—and their monolingual peers—are taught to see students' multilingual repertoires as liabilities rather than assets. In this chapter, we examine ways teachers can use literature to challenge monoglossic ideologies, promote rigorous learning, and affirm the identities, languaging, and value of plurilingual students and communities.

Scaffold 1: Exploring Plurilingual Poetry

In *El otro México*, a poetic representation of translanguaging, written years before the term itself was coined, scholar and activist Gloria Anzaldúa described the U.S.-Mexico border as a

> 1,950 mile-long open wound
> > dividing a *pueblo*, a culture,
> > running down the length of my body,
> > staking fence rods in my flesh,
> > splits me   splits me
> > > *me raja   me raja* (1987, p. 2)

From *Borderlands/La Frontera: The New Mestiza*. Copyright © 1987, 1999, 2007, 2012 by Gloria Anzaldúa. Reprinted by permission of Aunt Lute Books. www.auntlute.com

Newcomer and emergent plurilingual students are intimately familiar with borders; they cross geographic, political, linguistic, and social borders on a daily basis. By teaching poems like Anzaldúa's, teachers can not only invite conversations about students' experiences, but also explicitly position emergent plurilingual students as having unique and valuable insight regarding academic content. In Alison's classroom, she taught *El otro México* as part of a broader analysis of border-crossing in literature, examining questions like:

- Where does Anzaldúa use English, and where Spanish? Why?
- What is the emotional impact of the physical representation of words on the page?
- What borders does Anzaldúa cross? How does she feel about them? How do you know?
- What borders do you cross, encounter, or shy away from in your own daily lives?
- Which words and allusions are likely to be accessible to Spanish speakers from different regions of the world, and which will be unfamiliar? What does that mean about what it means to be "fluent" in a language?

For students like Alison's, who self-identified as "fluent" in Spanish but were unfamiliar with the unique geographic and linguistic nuances of Anzaldúa's (Chicanx) writing, poems like *El otro México* offer an opportunity to stretch their linguistic repertoire in both English and Spanish. Rather than positioning emergent plurilingual students as liabilities—or as linguistic resources to be "used" to support monolingual students—lessons like these enable teachers to transgress monoglossic ideologies and foster academically rigorous, dynamic learning among all students.

When reading *El otro México* with educators, we challenge them to consider the poem not only as a *testimonio* (testimony) to Anzaldúa's experience, but also to read it through their professional lenses. In classrooms, teachers often function as institutional gatekeepers who create and enforce linguistic borders, and even the most well-meaning educators sometimes perpetuate languaging practices that separate, regulate, or silence students. For example, many bilingual educators attempt to meet the "needs" of plurilingual students by repeating or translating written instructions into two languages. However, while translation does scaffold understanding among some students, it also can discourage students from experimenting with new ways of languaging, or marginalize students from other linguistic communities. Thus, we encourage teachers to rely less on direct translation and more on scaffolding understanding by drawing from multiple named languages (translanguaging), exploring connotation and detonation, using nonverbal representations, or using other practices that authentically stretch students' linguistic repertoires (see Chapters 6 and 7).

Throughout, we avoid reinforcing the social and geopolitical constructs that divide or create hierarchies within students' linguistic repertoires, such as labeling language as "L1" and "L2" or "home language" and "school language," and instead center students' development as emergent plurilingual students who are encouraged and have the freedom to use registers, idiolects, and nuances beyond political and linguistic borders. Anzaldúa (1987) explains this linguistic liberation, stating

> Until I am free to write bilingually and to switch codes without having always to translate, while I still have to speak English or Spanish when I would rather speak Spanglish, and as long as I have to accommodate the English speakers rather than having them accommodate me, my tongue will be illegitimate. (p. 81)

By framing students' linguistic repertoires and emergent plurilingualism as an asset, teachers can reinforce students' sense of identity and agency (Valenzuela, 2016). This enables students to experience their integration into U.S. schools and societies, and their development of subject area[7] English, as an additive, rather than subtractive, experience. In the words of one of our students, the Language Explorer programs

> . . . meant a lot for me because it was more about learn[ing] how [to] express myself in English without forgetting or being ashamed of my native language. [Before I came,] I did know how to speak [English] but not what or why.

Analyses of multilingual texts provide opportunities not only to use content that reflects students' experiences, but also to challenge them to become metacognitive about their languaging practices as they consider how and why authors draw from their full linguistic repertoires.

When designing professional learning for educators, we use poems like Anzaldúa's to model ways to ground our explorations of the lived experiences of students in the broader context of arts and literacy education. We use these conversations to (re)introduce teachers—many of whom teach math or science in their day-to-day classrooms—to the disciplinary language of literacy. We define and identify examples of figurative language in poetry, of patterns of rhyme, of sound devices like assonance and consonance. Similarly, as we sit with the violence of Anzaldúa's imagery—of fence rods staked down the narrator's flesh—we might invite teachers to contemplate contemporary images of our own countries' borders: the photographs of refugees seeking asylum, the walls, the protests, the children locked in detention, the hands held through the fences. We then use the disciplinary vocabulary of the arts to explore concepts like tone, imagery, composition, and symbolism. This act of teaching outside one's discipline isn't always comfortable for teachers, yet the disequilibrium it creates provides an invaluable opportunity to learn from and through teachers' collective creativity. Essentially, just as we ask students to share their own experiences as border crossers, so too do we invite teachers to cross the physical and metaphoric borders perpetuated within our classrooms, schools, and disciplinary structures.

CROSSING BORDERS WITH CHILDREN'S AND YOUNG ADULT LITERATURE

Over the years, we have used a wide array of children's and young adult literature, poetry, and graphic novels in the SLA (some of our favorites can be found at www.bravingup.com and at Teachers College Press at tcpress .com/dover-resources. In addition to being linguistically accessible to students who are developing their academic vocabularies in English, the illustrations in picture books and graphic novels—and the lush imagery of poetry—provide multiple entry points for linguistically diverse students.

For some teachers—especially those without training in the teaching of literacy and language arts—reading picture books with teenagers can feel like a risk: *Will students like them? Are they rigorous enough?* However, by strategically situating picture books within multimedia text sets related to core concepts, teachers are able to build lessons that are engaging and accessible, as well as both linguistically and academically robust.

As part of beginning-of-the-year activities, for example, teachers can read picture books like Choi's (2003) *The Name Jar* and Williams, Mohammed, and Stock's (2009) *My Name Is Sangoel* alongside poems like Tafolla's (1992) *In Memory of Richi* and Matam, Acevedo, and Yamazawa's (2014) *Unforgettable*. In addition to validating students' identities by honoring the importance of their names (e.g., see Kohli & Solórzano, 2012), texts like these provide a foundation for deeper discussions of personal and social identity as students tell the story of their own name, explore differences between the ways they are named by the world and how they choose to name themselves, or analyze how diverse students' names are treated within school settings.

In our Language Explorer classrooms, we typically pair children's books like Cisneros's (1994) *Hair/Pelitos* or Parr's (2009) *It's Okay to Be Different* with poetry and young adult novels such as Soto and Jenkins' (2009) poem *Ode to Family Photographs* or Yang's (2006) graphic novel *American Born Chinese*. Each of these engages themes related to how students appear on the outside versus how they feel internally, creating opportunities to address concepts as diverse as biology (e.g., genotype versus phenotype), family structure and diversity, and narrative style (omniscient versus limited narration, reliability of narration, etc.).

EXPLORING IDENTITY WITH ARTS-BASED PEDAGOGY

Scaffold 2: Split-Image Portraiture

For students who are border-crossers, navigating—and deciding how to narrate—their multiple countries, languaging, and identities can be complex. Thus, we use analyses of identity in children's and young adult literature as a springboard for conversations about students' own multiple and intersectional identities. Figures 5.1 and 5.2 illustrate how arts-based pedagogy can support students' reflection on themes of identity in literature and their own lives. Each of these examples emerged from lessons related to what we can learn about characters from looking at their "outsides" (what they explicitly say and do; how they look physically) and what we learn from their "insides" (what the narration reveals about their thoughts and motivations; what we can infer based on our reading).

Figure 5.1 depicts Jamal's "split-image portrait," which he drew after analyzing differences between how the central character in Yang's graphic novel *American Born Chinese* saw himself and how he was perceived by his peers. In this activity, students divide their portraits in half in order to simultaneously depict their outward and inner selves. Jamal chose to use an avatar to represent his physical features, then hand-drew images to show

Figure 5.1. Jamal's Split-Image Portrait

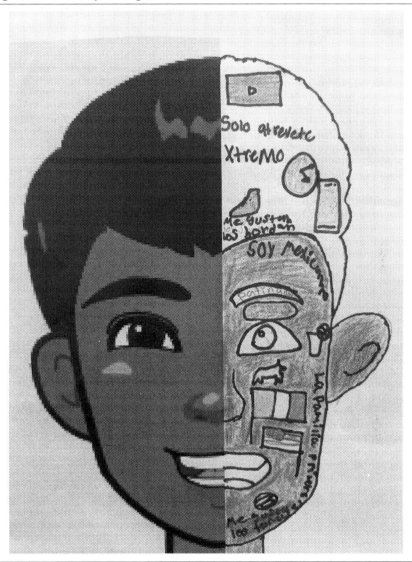

aspects of his identity that are hidden beneath the surface, including his cultural identities, hobbies, and aspirations.

In describing his self-portrait, another student, Esteban, said

I drew half my face on the paper to represent what people can see about me when they meet me. Then on the other half of the paper, I drew everything people can't see . . . I drew the Salvadoran

flag, and the U.S. flag [because] El Salvador is my country where
I was born in. I drew the U.S. flag because this country means a
lot to me. The U.S. has given me happiness, good experiences,
and opportunities that have helped me blossom. I also drew music
notes because I love music. I drew a graduation cap because I want
to graduate from high school and go to college. I drew a crawfish
and a crab because my favorite food is seafood. I drew a lion, my
favorite animal. I drew mountains because I love nature, and with
invisible pen I wrote my goals, accomplishments and words I feel that
represent me . . . *Gracias; lo apreciamos mucho.*

Many of our teachers use activities like this one to help students explore
themes of characterization, identity, assumptions, inference, and motivation.
As Esteban notes when describing his portrait, some teachers invited students to use invisible ink to depict their "internal monologues." Although
the invisible portions of students' portraits cannot be reproduced in this
book, in the classroom, when viewed under a blacklight, the images reveal
students' most secret inner thoughts. Esteban's self-portrait, for example, is a
pencil sketch, his cropped hair and strong brows the only distinguishing features on the left side of the page; brightly colored versions of the flags of the
United States and Mexico, accompanied by a cup of café con leche, adorn the
right. Under the black light, however, more of his story emerges: "[I think
of] soccer, *tacos, [y] México, porque es mi pais querido y que nunca voy a olvidar.*"[8]
The vulnerability with which Esteban describes Mexico and the depth of his
connection underscore the sacred nature of our students' identities, and the
tremendous imperative to welcome and affirm students' whole selves in our
classrooms.

Scaffold 3: Family Portraits

Newcomer and emergent plurilingual students enter our classrooms with
widely varied and geographically dispersed familial networks. As part of
our effort to learn about students' identities, we often invite them to create
portraits depicting their biological or chosen family. Over the years, these
have included people students live with, their ancestors, and families separated by distance or death but together in spirit. After reading Gary Soto's
poem, *Ode to Family Photographs,* one of our Language Explorers, Penelope,
chose to draw herself, her mother, and her father (Figure 5.2), focusing on
the "different eyes" that shape the way each member of her family sees the
world. Just in case viewers did not fully appreciate the importance of looking
beyond physical characteristics, Penelope added an annotation to reinforce

Figure 5.2. My Family's Eyes: A Portrait

Everybody in my family has different eyes. My dad's eyes is like a river flow slowly in the middle of the forest, because when I feel sad just look at his eyes everything around me become peaceful. But mom's eyes are so different, her eyes is like the color of milk coffee with ice but her eyes can make your heart melt in the winter and also make your life happier. And me, a simple person, but when you look at my eyes, in there have a lot of mysterious of my life.

that looking at her family picture isn't enough to truly know her, "because you won't know what I am thinking and feeling."

Activities like these offer pathways through which teachers can learn about, affirm, and engage the identities, self-concepts, and cultural and linguistic assets students bring to the classroom (Nieto, 2013; Rodríguez-Izquierdo, 2015).

Scaffold 4: Story Mapping

Given our students' identities as newcomers in both their local communities and their classrooms, it is unsurprising that narratives of border crossing and migration prove especially impactful. As we read books like Kuntz, Shrodes, and Cornelison's (2017) *Lost and Found Cat: The True Story of Kunkush's Incredible Journey*, which traces the true story of an Iraqi refugee family as they lose, and are reunited with, a beloved pet, or Colato Laínez and Lacámara's (2016) fictionalized portrayal of how a young child makes sense of the labels used to classify immigrants (*Mamá the Alien/Mamá la Extraterrestre*), teachers guide students in both documenting the events in the text and evaluating how their own experiences reflect those described in literature. Throughout, they might use maps to follow a character's journey or create timelines depicting the highs and lows they experienced; see the companion website for additional instructional resources related to these projects.

As with all classroom activities, Language Explorer educators use their own lives and art as models for students. In Figure 5.3, for example, preservice teacher Sabino Reyes shared some of the highs (travel, activism on behalf of immigrant rights) and lows (family medical crises) that impacted his journey.

Figure 5.3. Teacher-Created Personal Timeline

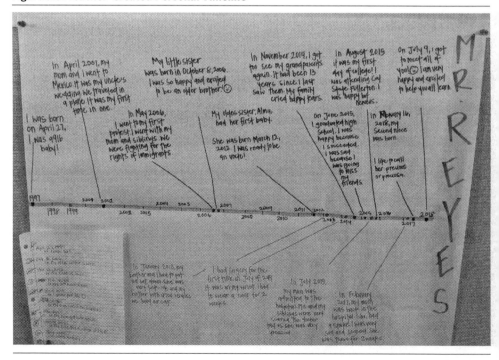

By bravely bringing their full, imperfect selves into the classroom, teachers can create welcoming spaces for students to share their own experiences; Sabino's student Cristopher, for example, created a life map featuring the lows of family separation to the joys of getting his first cow, learning to bike, and being reunited with his mother. Teachers can then use students' maps as a scaffold toward more complex written narratives; see "Using Children's and Young Adult Literature as a Springboard," below.

PUSHING BEYOND WORDS WITH PICTURE BOOKS

Scaffold 5: Literary Caminatas

Some picture books, such as Kim and Sánchez's (2015) *Here I Am*, present a unique opportunity to transcend languaging entirely. In this visual narrative, written wholly without words, a child and their family arrive in the United States only to encounter a dizzying array of unfamiliar foods, sounds, and streetscapes. Freed from the assumptions and boundaries created by an author's words in English, teachers invite students to take a critical *caminata* ("little walk") through the story, using visual clues to interpret the events. First, teachers read the book to the class, using a document camera to display each page; students take notes about key events, emotions, and images that they find striking. Next, teachers distribute one to two pages of the book to each student, and ask students with consecutive pages to gather in groups of three or four. Students then work together to decide how to use language to articulate characters' thoughts, feelings, and actions (Figure 5.4), before assembling their excerpts into a cohesive narrative (Figure 5.5). Additional resources related to critical caminatas are available at www.bravingup.com and via Teachers College Press at tcpress.com/dover-resources.

Each class invariably takes their narrative in a unique direction, creating opportunities for students to explore similarities and differences in their inferences and imaginings; during a recent caminata, for example, students noticed that classes interpreted the gender of the main character differently, sparking conversations about the gender-related norms, assumptions, and stereotypes that shaped students' reading of the text.

Figure 5.4. Writing Annotations for a Caminata

Figure 5.5. Assembling Annotations for *Here I Am*

Sample student annotation: "He is sad because he moved [out] of his country and because he's alone and everyone is playing behind him."

USING CHILDREN'S AND YOUNG ADULT
LITERATURE AS A SPRINGBOARD

Given the context of culturally and linguistically destructive schooling, creating affirming and engaging classrooms for newcomer students is a desirable outcome in and of itself. However, newcomer students deserve more than "just" affirmation; they also need a rigorous learning environment that prepares them to thrive throughout the academic year. Thus, we explicitly position our analyses of children's and young adult literature as springboards through which we teach the disciplinary language of literary analysis (characterization, symbolism, theme, plot, setting, etc.), and model skills like concept mapping, close reading, and annotation.

Scaffold 6: Concept Mapping

One of our Language Explorer teachers, Kristina, described her approach to using concept maps and visual organizers to prepare students to analyze and create narratives.

> In the morning, we did a free-write "I Am," and it talked about a struggle that the students have. Then we went ahead and did a reading from [Yang's] *American Born Chinese,* and then we discussed [as a] whole group some of the challenges that the kids faced [see Figure 5.6]. These are pretty typical of middle schoolers, I'd say!

After completing the group concept map, students selected a challenge that they themselves experienced; this would become the focus of their own narrative. Kristina and her co-teacher provided students with a comic-strip-style graphic organizer (see the companion website for a printable version of their template). "We had them do the first [panel] first," says Kristina, where they described their challenge, followed by the last panel. "Then they filled [in the middle] like a graphic novel. [At first] we focused more on the graphic part than the actual words, even though they have words." In this way, students use a combination of words and images to create an overarching general narrative; they then work individually and collaboratively to expand and revise their stories.

Figure 5.6. Sample Concept Map

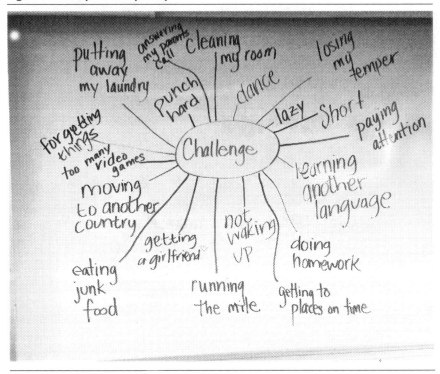

Scaffold 7: Journey Comics

In the Language Explorer classrooms, we often refer to these written and artistic narratives as "journey comics" for the way they function as maps of both the journeys of students' lives and the narrative arcs of their writing (see Figure 5.7). For example, in an early draft of a journey comic about soccer, Steven drew a series of panels featuring a single soccer player attempting, and failing, to make a goal. The only text in Steven's initial comic was a series of exclamations related to missed goals ("Oh man!" "That is closer!"); in the final panel the player celebrated a successful kick, saying "I kick harder because I practiced every day."

The final version of Steven's journey comic is far more detailed (see Figure 5.7). Titled "Steven Solves His Soccer Problem," the comic begins with an introduction to a "very bad defender" who "didn't know what to do." He is shown with tears streaming down his face; the narration describes him as sad and notes that "the coach always got mad at him because he's always scared." Unlike the first draft of his comic, which

Figure 5.7. Steven Solves His Soccer Problem

centered on the importance of practice, the final draft focuses on self-advocacy. In panel five, Steven speaks up for himself: "he told coach to change his position to striker." The coach agrees, but threatens to remove Steven from the game if he doesn't play well. In panels six and seven, we see Steven excel in his new position and celebrate with his team and family following the game.

In addition to deeper characterization and complexity, the final version of Steven's comic also provides evidence of his increasing fluency in the anatomy of graphic novels. It has a clear narrative arc (including a setup, conflict, and resolution), and uses multiple features of comic art, such as dialogue, narration, setting, artistic perspective, and facial expression, to convey characters' actions, experiences, and inner thoughts. In the coming chapters, we explore additional pedagogical strategies teachers can use to amplify students' voices, both within and beyond the classroom walls.

Resources and Reflective Activities for Chapter 5

- In this chapter, we described the importance of selecting literature (children's books, poetry) that educators and students can utilize as a platform to explore their identities. Too often, educators teach *to* their focal texts. In the Language Explorers, however, we think of text as a starting point and teach *from* it. How does this concept apply to the way you approach content in your own classroom? What do you teach to, and what do you teach from? How can you use text and other content as a springboard rather than a destination?
- In Figure 5.1, Jamal compares his visible and invisible identities. When you think about your own identities, which aspects of your identity are most visible to your students? How does it affect us when people fail to see—or we feel are forced to hide—parts of our identity?
- Figure 5.6 depicts a list of challenges identified by newcomer and emergent plurilingual middle schoolers. How does this list compare to what you might have anticipated? Are there challenges you or your students experience that are not included on this list? What factors might impact the challenges students name when doing activities like this one?
- Choose one of the poems or children's books referenced in this chapter, and analyze it with colleagues. How does the author use words and imagery to convey characters' identities, experiences, and emotions? What are similarities and differences between your chosen text and your own

experiences? What borders have each of you crossed in your personal and professional lives?

- Additional print and multimedia resources for teaching about linguistic, geopolitical, and social borders can be found at www.bravingup.com and Teachers College Press at tcpress.com/dover-resources.

CHAPTER 6

Can You Hear Me? Amplifying Student Voice Within and Beyond the Classroom

As educators, we are always seeking new ways to engage and amplify students' voices in our classrooms. We create "hooks" or icebreakers to use at the beginning of each class session; incorporate student-driven activities, contemporary media, and high-interest texts; and design each class around opportunities for students to work individually, share their ideas with a partner or in small groups, and participate in whole-class discussion or analysis.

Scaffold 1: Planning For Engagement

Through strategic planning about both content and pedagogy, teachers are able to engage students' plurilingual voices and support them in experimenting with new ways of expressing their thoughts visually and verbally. Figure 6.1 presents an example of how these principles manifest in a sample schedule from one of our Saturday programs for newcomer students; additional instructional resources related to each of the featured activities are available on the companion website at www.bravingup.com and Teachers College Press at tcpress.com/dover-resources.

Figure 6.1. Sample Daily Schedule

9:00–9:10   Welcoming & Icebreaker: Scavenger Hunt

Students "hunt" through classroom artifacts (in this case, student-created collages) for images related to sensory clues (something that smells good, is squishy, is sharp, etc.); this both prepares students for the daily learning activities and functions as a community-building activity.

(continued)

9:10–9:25	Whole-Group Warm-Up: What Do Feelings Sound Like?
	Teachers share sound clips and ask students to try to identify the sound and describe the feelings each sound elicits (e.g., baby crying, rain, cat purring).
	Group discussion: Does everyone's experience sound the same way? How do personal experiences or memories affect the way we feel about sounds? Do we name these sounds in the same way in all our languages?
9:25–10:00	Activity Block 1: Independent Work
	Students select an emotion word (from a prior lesson) and create a soundboard (a slide with 3–5 audio clips) to represent that emotion.
	Students describe their emotion and sounds in the speaker notes but do not name their emotion on the slide itself. Teachers challenge students to leverage their full linguistic repertoires in their descriptions—can they describe their emotions and sounds in multiple languages? Can they add an abstract image that represents their chosen emotion?
10:0–10:15	Movement Break
	Teachers play clips of different types of music and invite students to use words and movement to describe how each clip makes them feel.
10:15–11:00	Activity Block 2: Small-Group Work
	Students share their soundboard in groups of 2 or 3. Can their peers guess their emotion based only on the sounds? Which sounds are the most helpful cues? Why?
	Group discussion: If students were to record additional sounds from their lives, what would they be? What out-of-school sounds do students associate with these feelings?
11:00–11:30	Large-Group Sharing and Closing
	Students share one of their sounds with the large group.
	Exit ticket: Students write a plurilingual description of one of their sounds, describing the characteristics of this sound and why it represents their chosen emotion.

However, convincing students to speak is not enough; instead, we must also listen to what they say, and be accountable to the implications of their stories for our work as educators.

STUDENTS' VOICES TEACH US WHO THEY ARE

Every interaction we have with students presents an opportunity to learn about our newcomer students' cultural, linguistic, and educational journeys. In the classroom, we strategically scaffold learning activities to support students, from sharing superficial descriptions of their identities (e.g., based on what they like, how they look, and their hobbies) to presenting complex depictions of their multiple social, linguistic, and aspirational identities. These multilayered narratives offer windows into a community of students who are too often marginalized in mainstream schooling.

Scaffold 2: Exploring Languaging, Identity, and Community in Student Writing

As teachers gain experience braving up, they are able to more effectively support students in exploring their cultural and linguistic identities, life journeys, and innermost thoughts. Moreover, in addition to engaging newcomer and plurilingual students in classroom discourse, learning activities like autobiographical writing, self-portraits, collaborative poetry, and journey comics provide opportunities for teachers to learn about students' experiences of migration, approach to languaging, and family dynamics—many of which have a significant impact on their day-to-day classroom interactions. In the following section, we explore some of the stories that emerge in our newcomer students' writing, as well as the implications for teaching and learning.

Meet Paolo, Who Creates a Unique Story

Paolo entered the Language Explorers during his first year in the United States, and was both a cultural and linguistic minority within the community: as a native Brazilian and Portuguese speaker in a district where the overwhelming majority of newcomers and emergent plurilingual students were Spanish speakers from countries in Central America, Paolo felt both linguistically and socially isolated. (In fact, Paolo was the only Portuguese-speaking student we encountered in the 5 years we worked with his district.) Paolo's initial response to the question "Who are you?"—written entirely in English and in the third person—revealed the scope of his uncertainty about his place in his new community:

> [Paolo is] having some difficulties with who he is, because he still don't know. He miss who he was 2 years ago, because he knew who he was in the past and don't like who he is now as much he did before, but [he] is not sad at all! He

is happy, he has difficulties but don't see reason to be sad about that, [he] likes to solve problems, and he will solve this one too.

Paolo went on to say that his life was better in his home country, because he had two best friends (for which he was "proud of himself"), but did not have friends in the United States. In the days to come, Paolo continued to open up in the classroom, sharing details about his experiences. In the following excerpt from his "I Am" poem, written during his second week in the classroom, Paolo shares his identity as an artist and storyteller, strategically using his full linguistic repertoire to simultaneously reveal and conceal key elements of his narrative.

I am a creative artist, who creates a unique story.
I wonder nothing, I have dense and concrete thoughts so I have
     nothing to wonder about.
I hear my thoughts in my mind thinking about things around me.
I see my creations around me mixing with the real world.
I want to make my story real and the world to hear it.
I am a creative artist, who creates a unique story.
Eu finjo estar dentro das histórias que eu criei.
I feel happy and free when I create
. . .
I hope my dreams come to be real with my creations.
I am a creative artist, who creates a unique story.

Paolo's poem was written entirely in English, a language accessible to his teachers and some of his fellow students, with the exception of a single line: *"Eu finjo estar dentro das histórias que eu criei"* [I pretend to be inside the stories I create]. Paolo's use of Portuguese for this line was not accidental, but rather a conscious use of language to keep aspects of his identity "safe" or private; just as his fantasy world is a refuge where he can escape isolation, Portuguese offers an opportunity to speak without fear of judgment. Paolo's metacognition about the role of languaging was a dominant theme in his writing: he frequently reflected on his proficiency in English and Portuguese, his dream of being able to speak five languages, and his classroom experiences with languaging. "I'm very proud of my creativity and ability to learn languages . . . , [this class] helped me a lot, not about learn English, but about how to use it and also how to express myself."

Rather than avoiding, ignoring, or overlooking students' languaging practices, braving up requires teachers to interrogate them. We can ask questions like, How do students like Paolo strategically use language to convey the complexities of their identities and experiences (e.g., see the discussion of Gloria Anzaldúa's poem *El otro México* in Chapter 5)? How do students' languaging practices change when they discuss abstract versus concrete concepts? Thoughts versus feelings? Do students use different languaging norms when writing to different audiences, or about different members of their family or community? And, perhaps most importantly: how do students' languaging practices reveal their sense of engagement, connection, and safety within educational spaces?

This is not always an easy task; like Paolo, students sometimes share their most important revelations in registers or languages their teachers cannot access, thus requiring educators to stretch in order to meet the challenge. Other times, our students use our own insufficient expectations to trick us, offering shallow responses in a format they know we can comprehend. In those cases, is it our task to tease out the narratives beneath the surface so that we can walk with students as they learn to bravely speak their truths.

Meet Lucha, Who Holds Us in Her Heart

Lucha entered our Language Explorer classrooms 3 years after immigrating to the United States; however, while she had a more expansive English repertoire than many of her fellow newcomers, she was not thriving at her home academic campus. Her first reflective writing was approximately 10 sentences long and written entirely in English. In it, she talked about coming to the United States, and then being "in depression for the last 2 years for bad reasons." When asked to describe her identity, she said she hoped to be a police officer, and that "my English it's not really good but I keep trying hard for my dreams."

Lucha's early writing could be described as fitting the stereotypical narrative expected of newcomer students: she came to the United States, struggled, and had aspirations of learning English and having a career. She presented her story as a neat package, entirely in English and summarized concisely. As Lucha built relationships with her teachers and classmates, however, she gradually began to open up about her experiences with abusive relationships, troubled relationship with her mother, and deep admiration for her father. Moreover, with each revelation came new layers of linguistic sophistication. Unlike her introductory autobiography, Lucha's closing narrative was three full pages, written entirely in Spanish, and detailed the impact four weeks in the summer Language Explorer program had on her sense of worth and connection.

In Lucha's words:

> *Lo que sea pense que este verano estria abburido pero fue el mejor verano de mi vida. Conocia a muchas personas que ahora ocupan un lugar muy especial*

en mi corazon entre [she names her 3 teachers] *son unas grandes maestras que quisiera tenerías en mi escuela.*[9]

Lucha said her experience as a Language Explorer inspired her to make changes in her life by *"sacar a toda la gente toxia de mi vida,"*[10] especially since she met two other newcomer students who

son como las hermanas que nunca pude tener y les agradesco porque desde el dia que ellas dos llegarron a mi vida le pusieron una gran luz que nadia podra apagar ellas dos an vuelto a poner una sonrisa muy grande en mi rostro.[11]

For Lucha, who did not feel as if she had a healthy educational or social community at her home school, the relationships she built with other new-comer students and faculty were transformative; she ended her narrative with the hope that she would be able to maintain these new relationships throughout the academic year (which may be possible, as she and one of her closest new friends went on to attend the same high school).

AMPLIFYING STUDENT VOICES IN THE CLASSROOM AND THE SCHOOL COMMUNITY

As students gain confidence that their plurilingual voices will be welcomed and affirmed within the classroom, they become more willing to brave up and use their voices to ask for what they truly need. For many of our newcomer students, one of their most pressing needs is for schools that see and honor their identities and humanity. As much as students like Paolo and Lucha value the community created within the Language Explorer classrooms, they also describe feelings of isolation throughout the rest of the school year. During one of our midyear reunions, for example, Paolo reflected on the successes and challenges of high school: "I've liked a lot in my new school," he said. "I'm learning a lot, but at the same time, I feel kind of stuck. I can't see space for improvement, and I've been having difficulties making friends."

Rather than responding to comments like Paolo's on an individual level—as if his sense of isolation were a personal failing or unique circumstance—teachers have the opportunity to use them as springboards for analyzing the *institutional and systemic* factors that shape students' experiences. For example, in one of our partner school districts, we noticed a pattern where students who were socially and academically engaged during the summer Language Explorer program—a voluntary, non-credit-bearing experience—had erratic attendance and grades throughout the school year. Because our Language Explorer teachers had taken the time to authentically get to know students, this raised a flag: they knew their newcomer students

Figure 6.2. Newcomer Students Analyzing Strengths and Areas for Growth

had academic dreams and aspirations, and were both capable of and passionate about their learning. Thus, teachers opted to brave up and ask hard questions about students' experiences at school. They invited students to come together for a midyear reunion, and share their insight and analysis of the district's approach to engaging newcomer students (see Figure 6.2). Students' responses were enlightening and highlighted the breadth and depth of their vision for positive transformation (see Figure 6.3).

Unlike stereotypes of emergent plurilingual students, which typically emphasize what they do not have (i.e., fluency in English), conversations like these reveal students' commitment to their own education—and their desire to be a part of creating more affirming schools. Students yearn for teachers who share their languages, for opportunities to use their experiences to help other newcomer and emergent plurilingual students, and to

Figure 6.3. Students' Analysis of Systemic Factors That Affect Their Schooling

What does your school do well?
- *There helping us a escribir y a pronunciar las cosas y letras bien.*
- *Understanding ELPAC [the English Language Performance Assessments for California] and reviewing results to improve English*
- *Una de las cosas que la escuela ase bien es que no te ase sentir menos y ps te ayuda a que quando en tus idioma*
- *Hace bien enseñar los que no suben inglés ya que es un idioma complicado pero poco a poco se aprenden*
- *They teach well and they make feel comfortable in their classes and in the school*

How could schools better support newcomer students?
- *Poner un guia del mismo idioma del estudiante para que el se sienta comodo y sepa como funciona la escuela y las clases. [Another student offered a similar suggestion: Que cada alumno tenga un estudiante que lo ayude en aprender ingles.]*
- *Ayudar al estudiante que no abla ingles*
- *Que los maestros hablen diferentes idiomas o traductores, para ayudar a personas que hables diferentes idiomas.*
- *They can help by talking with them and asking if they need help.*
- *They could make them feel welcome at the school and help them with the english*
- *Para empezar ellos asen que te sientas comodo contigo mismo y ps ellos ensenan que podemos loytrar nuestros suenos esforsandonos*

What is your hope for the future as a leader within your school?
- *Usar lo que ilo ya aprendi para ayudar a los demos. Por ejemplo, traducirles, a leer, a hablar*
- *That they aprenden about themselves.*
- *PS Ya las ayudaria a que no se sientas mal cuando no puedas desir alogo de la forma correcta y es aunque es no las oyude del [unclear] yo ayudaria a que confier en eyos*
- *Les ayudaria con mis experiencias en el ingles y que no usaran google translate.*
- *To motive more students para que vengan al programa y hagan amigos.*

Students' verbatim responses to questions posed by their teachers; we left students' spelling and grammar as written for illustrative purposes. What do you notice about students' vision and approach to languaging? How are students drawing from and integrating their full linguistic repertoires? (See the Chapter 6 Resources and Reflective Activities for additional discussion of students' responses.)

share their strengths. It is not uncommon for Language Explorer students to request *more* programming, from weekly Saturday classes to monthly reunions where they can "talk about *paseos, cosas nuevas para hacer, o nuevos idiomas para aprender juntos.*" When educators brave up and invite students to be part of the conversation, we all can *aprender juntos.*

LEARNING WITH AND FROM STUDENTS

In far too many classrooms, learning is constructed as one-directional: teachers teach and students learn. Brazilian educator Paolo Freire famously referred to this as a "banking" approach to education, in which "knowledge is a gift bestowed by those who consider themselves knowledgeable upon those whom they consider to know nothing" (Freire, 1970/2000, p. 72). Despite movements toward more student-centered pedagogies, ultimately most educational experiences remain structured around the knowledge teachers want to impart to students.

In our Language Explorer classrooms, we seek to disrupt this process by creating multidirectional learning processes in which students learn from teachers, teachers learn from students, and students learn from one another. Some of this emerges naturally: in authentically plurilingual classrooms, each participant is positioned as an expert of their own linguistic repertoire, and invited—indeed, expected—to share their expertise with other members of the community.

In the early days of our programs, our curriculum focused heavily on affirming students' identities, inviting their stories, and amplifying their linguistic agency. Over time, however, our focus shifted from learning *about* students to learning *from* students, with the goal of reconstructing educational spaces as grounded in the values, perspectives, and insights of our culturally and linguistically diverse newcomers. We began to ask how our Language Explorers' experiences could—and should—shape "traditional" academic year instruction, how they could share their expertise with monolingual and monocultural classmates and teachers, and how they could co-construct educational policy and practice. Doing so required us to become more strategic about our curriculum and pedagogy and begin to incorporate youth-led inquiry, research, and analysis.

Scaffold 3: Participatory Action Research and Photovoice

Whether students are writing autobiographical poems (see Chapter 4), creating multilingual self-portraits (see Figure 3.1 and the discussion of micrography in Chapter 5), or mapping the stories of their lives (see

Chapter 5), narrative and artistic explorations of identity are common features of culturally and linguistically sustaining pedagogy. In addition to building community and affirming students' personal, cultural, and linguistic assets, they center students' agency as they make creative decisions about how to reveal their identities, leverage their full linguistic repertoire, and act as author-director of their own *testimonios*.

Thus, when we wanted to incorporate research into our Language Explorer classrooms, we gravitated toward participatory, arts-based research methods, such as photovoice. Photovoice is a type of participatory action research where participants tell the stories of their lives through photographs, narratives, and public presentations—essentially using photographs to "voice" their experiences. Research attests to its efficacy in engaging newcomer, immigrant, and emergent bilingual youth in narrating their own cultural, sociolinguistic, and educational experiences, as well as the potential of photovoice projects to shift deficit discourses regarding historically marginalized students (see Delgado, 2015; Fruja Amthor & Roxas, 2016; Roxas & Gabriel, 2016; Roxas, Gabriel, & Becker, 2017; Zenkov & Harmon, 2009).

Photovoice projects provide opportunities for students to strategically create and curate artistic and narrative data about their identities and communities, and then present these data to outside audiences (such as peers, teachers, and district administrators). However, they also present challenges: in addition to inviting students to take and share pictures, teachers must find ways to ensure students do not merely create collages, but instead compose, capture, and strategically use images to write a cohesive, intentional, and authentic narrative. Thus, we recommend teachers prepare for photovoice projects by engaging students in the analysis of diverse aspects of identity and culture, as well as artistic and linguistic elements of visual storytelling.

For example, since few of our Language Explorers students have training in photography or visual arts, we began our photovoice journey by walking students through the process of analyzing images in children's books, graphic novels, or murals. In Chapter 5, we present our approach to using critical caminatas to support students' analysis of picture books; during other years, we have focused on how authors and artists use images in graphic novels (such as Yang's *American Born Chinese* and Telgemeier's [2016] *Ghosts*), comics, and street art in our local community (see Figure 6.4).

Throughout, teachers coach students in examining the composition of the work, asking questions like: What draws your eye? What is in the foreground? What is in the background? What do you think the artist or photographer *wants* you to focus on when you look at this image?

Students then shift from the role of audience to that of creator, as they take a series of pictures that offer a *ventana* (window) into their lives and communities. In addition to providing insight into students' out-of-school

Figure 6.4. Analyzing Imagery in Children's Books

Teacher Shawna Dinnen guides students in analyzing a scene from Kuntz, Shrodes, and Cornelison's (2017) *Lost and Found Cat: The True Story of Kunkush's Incredible Journey.*

lives, visual expressions like photography enable emergent plurilingual students to construct and curate their stories, while simultaneously functioning as scaffolds that facilitate plurilingual languaging and support students in expressing abstract and concrete ideas (Chen, 2020). When students first bring their photographs to class, teachers invite them to label elements and themes in their photographs (see Figure 6.5) and use graphic organizers (such as Venn diagrams) to identify similarities and differences between their photos and those of their peers. Students' initial annotations are typically simple: *es el parque; this is my school; here is my family.*

As students share and compare their images, we challenge them to be metacognitive about the stories they are telling: What are they hoping to show about their community? Do they want to focus on physical aspects of their community or neighborhood? The people and cultural practices that surround them? Strengths or tensions that affect their experiences as newcomers? Students then begin to build their initial labels into more comprehensive annotations ("This picture shows a park in my community . . . [it] is important to me because I came here with my dad and sister, Aurora, to

Figure 6.5. Exploring Concrete and Abstract Images in Photographs

play . . . The events we have celebrated in the park are many birthdays."). We then incorporate activities such as physical or virtual "gallery walks," where students ask questions of and make comments regarding peers' images, to support students in focusing not only on the "what" that is depicted in each image, but on how they can use visual media to tell complex, situated, and multifaceted stories about their identities and experiences.

The following excerpts are examples of students' final photovoice annotations, as they presented them at a community forum for their parents, teachers, and district officials:

> I see the house, I see the tree around the house . . . I see the persons is live in this house are good persons . . . This is my house,

also I like the people in my house and where I live. This is important because this represent my life, my culture, who I am.

This school is very important as it is my school where I am currently studying and where I met my first friends in this country . . . this school gave me the opportunities to go back to school because in my country I could not continue studying [because] of gangs . . . I had to emigrate to this country leaving my family friends and everything . . . This photo symbolizes hope in my life and to be able to study since . . . everything was lost to me and although it was very difficult to get here but here I am with a hope to fulfill my dreams.

Esta foto es cuando salí de la escuela, ese momento nunca lo olvidaré porque pasé muchos momentos felices con mis amigos y maestros cuando dejé la escuela. Estaba muy triste y feliz porque conocería más escuelas pero extrañaría a mis amigos y profesores. Ese día mis amigos y yo comenzamos a bailar hasta que el baile terminó. Todos mis amigos llevaban vestidos y vi que muchos niños de octavo grado comenzaron a llorar e iba a llorar porque algunos de mis amigos salen a otras escuelas, y otros salen a México con sus padres.[12]

In addition to honoring and affirming students' agency and authority to write their own stories, the public nature of photovoice projects creates opportunities for educators to truly listen to students' voices. We find that teachers and district administrators are sometimes surprised by what they see and hear, as students challenge the preconceptions or stereotypes that even experienced, well-intentioned educators bring to their work with newcomers. In the words of Language Explorer teacher Angelique, students' projects reinforced that newcomers are

. . . ambitious students who valued their education and really wanted to become proficient in English. Unfortunately, students like Luca, Thai, Alex and Amir—my students—are ignored and left voiceless in traditional classrooms, when I know they have powerful voices that deserve to be heard.

While the teachers who work with our Language Explorer programs are typically teachers who, like Angelique, are authentically interested in listening to and learning from newcomer students, the reality is that most institutionalized educational systems are not built to center the interests and priorities of emergent plurilingual students. Newcomer and emergent plurilingual students rarely have a place within the governance or leadership of school communities (such as the student government) and are often absent from the most academically rigorous pathways within the school (such as Advanced Placement or honors programs; see Estrada, 2014; Solórzano & Ornelas, 2002; Thompson, Umansky, & Porter, 2020). Moreover, there are often significant cultural, linguistic, and socioeconomic differences between a district's "elite" students and its newcomer and emergent bilingual students—and few opportunities for students, and teachers, to come together across this divide.

Thus, if we wish to truly brave up and create radically inclusive educational spaces, we must not only listen to and learn from students, but also act upon their vision and recommendations. In the coming chapters, we examine how teachers and administrators can work collaboratively with newcomer and emergent plurilingual students as they navigate social and educational crises (Chapter 7), challenge monoglossic approaches to assessment (Chapter 8), and institutionalize culturally and linguistically sustaining policy and practice (Chapter 9).

Resources and Reflective Activities for Chapter 6

- In this chapter, we see the ways students like Paolo strategically use languaging to reveal and conceal aspects of their identities. How do you see students do this in your own context? How do you feel and respond when students speak and write in languages you do not know?
- How does your school site solicit student and community input regarding educational policies and practices? Whose voices, and languages, are invited, affirmed, amplified, and silenced during conversations about curriculum, pedagogy, and leadership? Are newcomer students and families invited to merely "participate" or give "feedback," or are there authentic opportunities for students to co-create agendas, identify priorities, and shape policy? What can YOU do differently to promote a more equitable, heteroglossic approach?
- In Figure 6.3, we include excerpts of students' verbatim analysis of systemic factors that affect their schooling as written in both English and Spanish. If you are not a Spanish speaker, what are the strategies and scaffolds you used to read students' responses? How did you draw upon your existing linguistic repertoire while reading? How did the call to make meaning of a text written in a language you do not speak impact you emotionally? How did it stretch your linguistic, professional and pedagogical resources?
- Additional resources for teaching with sound and using photovoice can be found on the companion website at www.bravingup.com and Teachers College Press at tcpress.com/dover-resources.

CHAPTER 7

And Then We Had to Pivot: Bringing Culturally and Linguistically Sustaining Teaching Online

Nobody was prepared for the COVID-19 pandemic, nor for its dramatic impact on teaching and learning. Seemingly overnight, students and teachers alike had to "pivot" as schools closed, districts scrambled to provide technology and Wi-Fi, and students disappeared from classrooms by the dozen. In the months after schools closed, Los Angeles Unified School District—one of our neighboring school districts—reported that tens of thousands of students were either missing from their online classrooms or checking in only periodically (Besecker & Thomas, 2020). Unsurprisingly, attendance patterns both reflected and exacerbated racial and linguistic inequities: during the first 3 months of the school closures, there was a 20-percentage point differential between online participation rates of Asian American and White students and their Black and Latinx peers; poor and working-class students were 10% less likely to participate in online learning than their wealthier peers. According to LAUSD data, 40% of Emergent Plurilingual students logged into online classes less than once per week, a rate 20% lower than that of their English-proficient peers (Besecker & Thomas, 2020; California Alliance of Researchers for Equity in Education, 2020).

In thinking about these data, it is essential to consider it within its broader context; these attendance patterns don't suggest that newcomer and emergent plurilingual students "opted out" of online schooling, but rather that they were disproportionately impacted by resource inequities, from the nature of their out-of-school learning environments, to their access to technological resources required for online learning, to the availability of affirming and linguistically accessible online learning. For example, according to data from the 2018 Census and National Center for Education Statistics, approximately 30% of all U.S. public school students live in households without an Internet connection or a device adequate for distance learning at home, and of these, more than half live in households with neither an adequate connection nor an adequate device for distance learning (Chandra, Chang, Day, Fazlullah, Liu, McBride, Mudalige, & Weiss, 2020). Teachers, too, struggled with connectivity, with approximately 300,000 to 400,000 public school teachers (8%) lacking access to adequate connectivity to teach effectively from home (Chandra et al., 2020). Unsurprisingly, lack of connectivity has a disproportionate impact on students and educators in lower socioeconomic communities, as well as communities of color, migrant communities, and emergent plurilingual students (U.S. Department of Education, 2019). All of this took place within the broader context of pandemic-related inequities, from gross disparities in incidence of COVID-19 infection and death, to trends associated with household density and opportunity to work from home, to pandemic-related economic factors (e.g., Artiga, Corallo, & Pham, 2020; Esquivel & Blume, 2020).

Even in districts that are deeply attuned to the needs of newcomer students—like those with whom we are privileged to work—systemic issues had a dramatic impact on students' daily experiences. In the words of Language Explorer teacher Rene,

> Although the district and federal government dedicated money and supplies to bridge this gap, it became glaringly obvious that mostly Hispanic students needed devices and mobile hotspots. By the time students received a working device and/or hotspot, it was the end of the academic year for 2019–2020. Once the district came to the decision that they were going to remain 100% virtual for the Fall semester, they started passing out more devices and hotspots to not only students, but teachers. Once again, there wasn't enough money or resources dedicated to the infrastructure and our online LMS system, school websites, and internet consistently crashed the first 2 months of school. The constant interruption was very frustrating for students, parents, and teachers.

Our years of work with newcomer and emergent plurilingual students underscore the tremendous commitment students—and their families—make to their education. We saw this dedication on a daily basis, as students emailed (and messaged, and texted) to check in or request the access and supports they needed. We saw nothing short of Herculean efforts on the part of students and families; when necessary, our students attended class from cars, public parks, fast food restaurants, and shelters. They learned in the presence of parents, siblings, cousins, grandparents, and young children—all of whom periodically joined in during class discussions! They came to online classes from bedrooms, busy kitchens, front stoops, and occasionally the solace of the bathroom. Our Language Explorers braved up and used their voices to advocate for their educational journeys. However, students' perseverance and self-advocacy were far from enough to ensure equitable access to virtual schooling; even those students who were able to log into districts' online platforms were too frequently met with curriculum and pedagogy that failed to "see" them as students.

In the words of some of Language Explorer students: "my [math] teacher only speaks in English, if I ask for help they don't help me;" "they tell me to get things [supplies or materials] for school but I don't have them [at home];" "I did my work but then they said it was wrong" [this comment referred to homework that students completed, but submitted in the incorrect format—for example, if students did homework on paper but were required to submit it electronically]. In describing her students' daily experiences, Rene noted that

> Overall, our emergent bilingual students' online learning experience depended greatly on whether or not their teacher actually remembered they have EL [English Learning] students in their classes. Many teachers moved too quickly from page to page and [students] couldn't keep up or everything was a verbal lecture without textual support. Students were very confused and frustrated because they didn't know how to improve their grades.

Statewide research indicates these experiences were far from unique; during the first months of the pandemic, only 31% of California parents said their school was providing instructional materials for English learners, and 25% reported that their school had not provided *any* materials in languages other than English (Costa, 2020). Moreover, in an effort to implement "high-interest" online content, many districts turned to commercially produced resources; however, these are overwhelmingly available in English only and may not be culturally and linguistically representative, further marginalizing newcomer and emergent plurilingual students (Archambault, Shelton, & McArthur, 2021; California Alliance of Researchers for Equity in Education, 2020). The impact was rapid and dramatic; one year into the pandemic, 42% of the grades received by Los Angeles Unified School District's emergent plurilingual students were D's or F's, and internal assessment data indicated that 94% of the district's emergent plurilingual students were scoring below grade level in reading and math (Esquivel, 2021).

Data like these are shocking, and it is unsurprising to see headlines focused on "learning loss" and remedial solutions. However, it is important to put these data in context; grades and standardized tests are far from equitable, comprehensive, or conclusive measures of student learning. Everyone knows that students learned far more—about life, about themselves, about our society—during the COVID-19 pandemic than can ever be measured by a standardized assessment or tracked in a learning management program. Nevertheless, indicators like grades and test scores do point toward disparities in which students were—and were not—served by online schooling. Moreover, research suggests that simply knowing that they were labeled as "failing" affects students' sense of academic worth and future progress (e.g., Papay, Murnane, & Willett, 2010). We worry about the implications of pandemic-associated inequities for students' self-concepts. We wonder how test scores and grades will affect future educational offerings: Will districts require students to enroll in remedial coursework, thus limiting their future academic options? Or will they see these data as a sign of their *own* failure, and use the data as an opportunity to implement transformative pedagogies that authentically engage students' academic, cultural, and linguistic interests, needs, and priorities?

HUMANIZING ONLINE LEARNING

In Chapter 2, we described some of the ideological and pedagogical principles that ground our practice, including a commitment to culturally sustaining pedagogy (Paris & Alim, 2017), translanguaging and heteroglossia (Flores & García, 2013), and emergent curriculum (Dover & Schultz, 2018). These approaches paid off; during the first months of the pandemic, students in our Language Explorer programs described our classrooms as one of the only educational spaces in which they felt affirmed. Part of this was due to teachers' efforts to brave up throughout the academic year; students and teachers already had robust, reciprocal relationships, and students had *confianza* (confidence) that they would be seen, heard, and valued. Our teachers' efforts to create classrooms that functioned as humanizing spaces (Bartolomé, 1994; Freire, 1970/2000) built a foundation on which students, teachers, and families could work collaboratively to find ways to navigate the pandemic.

Nevertheless, the transition to online and distance-based learning created new challenges for newcomer and emergent plurilingual students and teachers. Students entered classrooms battered by the realities of living through a pandemic, with scars from their daily experiences with medical, financial, political, and educational trauma. As weeks rolled into months, it became clear that we needed to do more than "pivot" to online teaching; we would need to recommit to braving up in order to meet the tremendous challenges created and exacerbated by the pandemic. We wanted our classrooms to be more than spaces where newcomer and emergent plurilingual students could simply *access* learning; instead, we sought to create environments that built on the successes of our face-to-face Language Explorer programs and addressed the unique challenges of teaching wholly online.

Early in the pandemic, equity-oriented advocacy organizations, including the California Alliance of Researchers for Equity in Education (CARE-ED, 2020) and New York University's Metropolitan Center for Research on Equity and the Transformation of Schools (n.d.) issued a series of recommendations to guide educators in promoting culturally and linguistically sustaining teaching in online and distance-based classrooms. These include emphases on: (a) building relationships with students; (b) creating an affirming virtual and interpersonal community; (c) modeling flexibility of deadlines, format, and technology; and (d) explicitly engaging locally relevant questions of identity, equity, and justice. The U.S. Department of Education's Institute of Education Sciences amplified these commitments with recommendations to focus on student and family voice, collaborative and sustaining relationships, and social justice curriculum throughout the pandemic (Holquist & Porter, 2020). Similarly, Californians Together, a statewide coalition that advocates for emergent plurilingual students and policies, published a series of indicators related to linguistically inclusive online learning (Williams, 2020); these emphasize the importance of synchronous interaction, pedagogical supports for emergent plurilingual students, access to technological resources, family engagement, and social-emotional supports.

Prior to the COVID-19 pandemic, our Language Explorer classrooms already embodied many of these principles. In addition to an emphasis on community partnerships and inclusion, the Language Explorer programs have historically been both arts- and tech-rich, with opportunities for students to use an array of tools to plan, create, illustrate, annotate, and demonstrate their learning. Our teachers had experience thinking about when and how to use technology to amplify the voices of newcomer and emergent bilingual students; this creativity and flexibility would prove invaluable in the face of COVID-19. Nevertheless, this work would prove *hard*. There were days when online classrooms fell silent, when students went absent, when screens were blank, when teachers celebrated a student's creative use of (trans)languaging only to find their comment was cut-and-pasted from Google Translate.

In the pages that follow, we highlight strategies teachers can use to engage, encourage, and amplify learning when teaching newcomer and emergent plurilingual students in online classrooms, focusing both on pedagogical approaches and the rationale behind them; additional resources are available on the companion website at www.bravingup.com and at Teachers College Press at tcpress.com/dover-resources. Throughout, we wish to emphasize that whether face-to-face or online, *braving up* is not about adopting a specific set of tools or classroom activities, but rather about creating and affirming schooling as a space where students can bring their full humanity—their personal and cultural identities, their linguistic repertoires, their individual curiosities, and their academic priorities. That vision, more than any specific resource or assignment, must be the guiding principle behind our practice.

BREAKING THE SILENCE: ENGAGING STUDENTS AND BUILDING COMMUNITY

Before the COVID-19 pandemic, we thought we knew how to work with silence, both practically (through classroom activities and icebreakers) and metaphorically (by amplifying students' voices and agency). Nevertheless, teaching online changed the landscape entirely; teachers were suddenly talking to themselves in the presence of 30 small black Zoom boxes, an experience commonly called "teaching into the void." In many school districts, including those where we host Language Explorer programs, students were not required to turn on their cameras; though this was an effective way to mitigate some of the many issues of equity associated with online learning (from insufficient bandwidth to fears that one's learning environment would be judged by peers), it made it difficult to build community.

Language Explorer teacher Lê described how the shift to online teaching impacted the students in her science classes:

This past year I had 7 different languages spoken by students: Sinhala, English, Spanish, Vietnamese, Tagalog, Hindi, Arabic. My newcomer students included one student from Sri Lanka (who speaks Sinhala), one student from the Philippines (who speaks Tagalog), one student who spent much of the year in Kuwait (who speaks Arabic), and one student from Vietnam (who speaks Vietnamese). I had several students who speak Spanish and are newcomers, and many students who are not newcomers but fluid bilinguals in Spanish. I had one student who has lived here for many years now and speaks Hindi, but was very proud of her Hindi and wanted it to be included as much as possible when I was translating into languages other than English . . .

[Some of my students] thrived in online learning. They came to the United States with their entire family, and their parents would sit with the student during classes and help their student with translating . . . [other students struggled. One student] told me that when they lived in Vietnam, they were friends with everybody in their class. But here, they didn't know anyone . . . I tried to introduce my [Vietnamese-speaking] students from last year to the student from this year, and it was fun; however, I didn't know how to create the space for them to have unstructured, authentic friendships.

Indeed, the concept of unstructured, authentic interactions would prove among the most difficult to nurture in online classrooms. Unlike face-to-face classrooms, where students are active members of the learning community from the moment they walk through the door, students sometimes experience online classrooms as waiting rooms, where they passively bide their time until they are told what task they have to accomplish. Thus, teachers must find a way to interrupt the passivity of video learning and invite students to build and engage with each other in a virtual space.

In our face-to-face Language Explorer classrooms, educators are very intentional about how they arrange and decorate their classrooms; on Day 1, most rooms will include photos related to educators' identities and cultures, bulletin boards or butcher paper for word walls, and teacher-created models of major projects. Teachers carefully plan how they will welcome students into this new learning environment: What words, images, and languages will be visible as students approach the doorway? What music will be playing as they enter the room? What will students do as they wait for others to arrive? How will they get to know one another, even when they don't share a common named language? Then, as students write, create art, and share photographs and cultural artifacts, the walls come alive; essentially, students collaboratively rebuild a physical classroom that reflects their unique and robust cultural and linguistic community.

Co-creating the classroom community can be more challenging in a virtual space, where teachers (now repurposed as "meeting hosts") have sole control over the physical environment and artifacts disappear each time they change the slide. In order to disrupt the sterility of online spaces, educators can engage students in co-creating their learning environment through the use of plurilingual playlists featuring students' favorite songs, the inclusion of student work on an ever-evolving virtual background, and invitations to co-design and co-host welcoming and break-time activities.

Scaffold 1: Icebreakers and Community-Building

Searching for "virtual icebreakers" returns dozens, if not hundreds, of recommendations; "would you rather" polls, activities where students choose which cat meme best represents their feelings, games of two-truths-and-a-lie, virtual Pictionary, online polls, scavenger hunts, virtual dance parties, and collaborative jigsaw puzzles are only some of the dozens of icebreakers our teachers have tried. One class of Language Explorers was so enthusiastic about the multiplayer social deduction game *Among Us* that students started arriving earlier and earlier to maximize game time! These types of playful activities are invaluable tools for building community.

In general, we consider any icebreaker that gets students interacting successful; however, some activities have the added benefit of not only engaging students but also serving as authentic scaffolds toward creating brave, affirming, and plurilingual classrooms. These are some of our favorites; see the companion website for additional examples and resources to support instruction.

Placing Ourselves on the Map

Display an editable map of the world, and invite students to place a pin in a location that is important to them and add an audio or written explanation of its importance. Students share their locations with the class and identify common themes across students' selected sites (e.g., did they choose their home country? A place in nature? Somewhere where someone they love lives?). In some Language Explorer classrooms, teachers and students continued to annotate their shared map, adding additional pins (for locations mentioned in literature, home countries of artists and activists they studied, etc.) or video or sound clips to help other students "feel" important places, or creating fictitious routes connecting students' favorite places.

Plurilingual Feelings Wheels

As students enter the virtual classroom, show an example of a plurilingual feelings wheel or nonverbal emoji board (see the companion website at www.bravingup.com for resources). Challenge students to select a word or image that describes how they are feeling, then find a similar but not identical word on the board. Students share the two words, and explain why they chose one word over the other. As an extension, students can work in groups to create a communal collage of images and GIFs related to the emotion of their choice; other students can then try to guess the emotion and explore cultural and linguistic nuances related to expression.

Student Work Scavenger Hunts

Select examples of student-created art or plurilingual poetry to display as a slide or virtual background; we especially like using students' nametags, micrography, and split image portraiture for this activity (see Chapters 3 and 4). Invite students to "scavenge" their peers' work for examples of concepts discussed in class (a symbol, an example of translanguaging, a shared characteristic, deep or surface aspects of culture, etc.) or unique uses of literal or metaphorical language (e.g., something "shady" or something inspiring).

Virtual Lockers

Use an online template to create a virtual "locker room" (see Figure 7.1) in which students post avatars, photographs, favorite songs and movies, and artifacts from their out-of-school lives. Students share their lockers in small groups, using Venn diagrams (on paper or via an app like Google Jamboard) to identify ways they are similar to and unique among their peers; teachers can then use students' lockers as a springboard for building community, exploring language (e.g., through plurilingual annotation), and identifying contextually resonant themes. For example, the commentary in Figure 7.1 is as follows:

> My locker has pictures of my daughters (age 7 & 11), husband, moms, and puppy, as well as pics from when I brought students to Spain last year and a family camping trip.
>
> I love to read, so there are lots of books in my locker, including a Spanish textbook (porque estoy practicando mi español académico) and the book I wrote, as well as others that impacted me.
>
> Towards the bottom of my locker, there are links to two of my favorite songs, "Nuvole Bianche" by Ludovico Einaudi and "Wrote My Way Out" from the Hamilton Mix Tape (I love the idea of writing setting us free)
>
> Other images represent my love of biking and cooking (mostly vegetarian), commitment to social and racial justice, and artifacts related to the pandemic. The flowchart poster was created by a friend of mine early in the pandemic, and basically says that if your children aren't actively on fire, you're doing okay at balancing everything during the pandemic. This is something I'm trying to remember.

See the companion website for templates and instructional resources related to teaching with virtual lockers.

Say What? Starting with Spoken Word

In an effort to interrupt the monolingual, monoglossic lens common among commercialized curriculum, poets, artists, and educators have published an array of plurilingual, interactive, and high-interest spoken word libraries, including the #TeachLivingPoets Virtual Library (https://teachlivingpoets .com/virtual-library/) and the LatiNext Poetry Project (http://bit.ly/LatiNext

Figure 7.1. A Virtual Locker Created by Author Alison Dover

_Lessons). In this icebreaker, teachers invite students to select a poem and choose a single "favorite line" to share with a small group of their peers. Each group then votes on and shares their favorite line with the full class, and the winning poem is played aloud for the group. In addition to diversifying the voices and languages privileged in the classroom, such activities are effective ways of introducing key concepts (e.g., through spoken word about linguistic inclusion, environmentalism, or racial identity) and engaging students' curiosity about poets' strategic use of languaging.

Scaffold 2: Supporting Online Discussions

Teachers who are new to online teaching sometimes expect virtual discussions to follow similar patterns as face-to-face discussions, except that they happen through video rather than in a physical classroom. We have not found this to be the case, as technical issues (such as audio delays), difficulties hearing multiple voices simultaneously, limited nonverbal signals, and the inevitable multitasking disrupt conversational flow. Thus, instead of trying to replicate face-to-face discussions, teachers must strategically leverage the opportunities and challenges of online communication.

For example, asynchronous conversations (whether written or spoken) offer emergent plurilingual students the opportunity to plan and rehearse their comments. For many students, practicing what they'd like to say before speaking in a larger group can help build confidence, enabling them to use language in ways that feel "risky." Similarly, students who are already comfortable enacting a specific type of productive literacy can use asynchronous conversations to explore new ways of using their linguistic repertoire; for example, we sometimes ask students to brainstorm two different ways they might phrase their comment, and then tell us how they decided which one to use. It is important to note, however, that some students experience asynchronous conversations as overly formal and are reluctant to participate unless they think their speech is "perfect," "appropriate," or "correct" (a construct that too often results in monolingual phrases created using Google Translate or similar services). See Chapter 8 for additional discussion of how to encourage linguistic experimentation and complexity without reinforcing language standardization.

Overall, braving up requires teachers—and students—to be willing to experiment with a wide array of conversational techniques and tools. No one strategy will work for all students, and experience demonstrates that a discussion strategy that worked well one day may flop entirely the next. Thus, in preparing to scaffold, facilitate, and deepen virtual discussions, we find it useful to focus both on the purposes of students' communication—is the goal to build community? explore ideas? assess students? prepare for presentations?—as well as the diverse productive literacies they seek to nourish (oral, written, and artistic; rehearsed and spontaneous; individual and collaborative; formal and informal; etc.). Having a clear sense of purpose will help teachers decide which pedagogies and scaffolds to use in a given discussion.

As our Language Explorer classes transitioned online, teachers incorporated a wide array of synchronous and asynchronous discussions into each lesson. These generally featured a warmup activity/icebreaker, individual brainstorming, paired dialogue, small-group activities, large-group discussions, and individual reflection.

In addition to using breakout groups for think-pair-share and small-group conversations, teachers can use platforms like Jamboard, Google Docs, Flipgrid, and text-based messaging to engage students in synchronous and asynchronous written, audio, and video conversations; written conversations, especially, create opportunities for students to translate among multiple languages, thus creating bridges among students without overlapping linguistic repertoires. Many of the tools we use in face-to-face plurilingual classrooms, such as word walls, sentence frames, discussion webs, and graphic organizers, can be easily adapted for online use. Figures 7.2 and 7.3 illustrate some of the ways Language Explorer teachers used online tools to support plurilingual students in exploring language and preparing for discussion.

Figure 7.2. Language Explorer Students Annotating a Virtual Word Wall (Padlet)

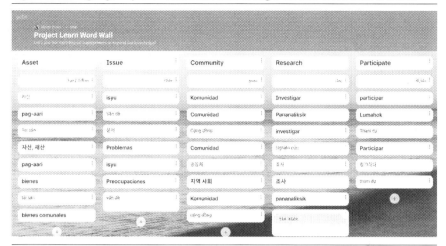

A plurilingual word wall created using Padlet. Later in the Language Explorer program, students would append images and videos to further illustrate key concepts.

Figure 7.3. Concept Map Exploring Personal Identity

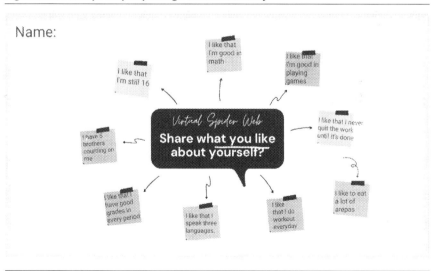

Example of a concept map created in Jamboard.

In addition to providing cognitive tools, linguistic scaffolds, and time for students to prepare for conversations in pairs or small groups, teachers must find ways to elicit, nourish, and sustain whole-class discussions. This objective has proven the most difficult aspect of implementing the Language Explorer program online: invariably, some students—and some languages—dominate, while other students are reluctant to participate in large-group synchronous conversations. Strategies like "waterfall chats" (where all students type a response in the chat, then simultaneously hit "send" when directed by the teacher) or discussion webs can both encourage participation by a greater number of students and offer opportunities for analyses of conversation patterns. Figure 7.4 is an example of how one Language Explorer teacher mapped students' participation during a synchronous conversation about social identity.

During this discussion, Language Explorer teacher Isaac Sanchez drew an arrow from the name of each speaker to the name of the person who spoke after them. At the conclusion of the discussion, he led students in an analysis of the conversation patterns (that teachers spoke more than anyone else; that some students never spoke to each other; etc.). Teachers can use activities like this to help students become metacognitive about communication patterns, challenge students to sustain discussion without teacher participation, and build classroom conversations that include all students.

Figure 7.4. Web Illustrating Students' Contributions During a Virtual Discussion

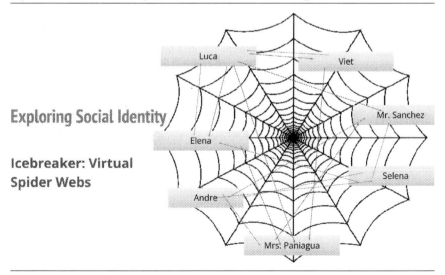

Scaffold 3: Modeling

One of the core tenets of the Language Explorer programs—whether face-to-face or online—is that our teachers never ask students to do anything they have not done themselves. This is invariably a risk, as many teachers enter the program with little or no experience writing poetry, drawing self-portraits, sketching autobiographical comics, creating movies, or candidly sharing their multiple social identities with colleagues or students. As teacher educators and project coaches, we model self-disclosure, linguistic fluidity, and creative expression throughout pre-program professional learning sessions, using examples of our own poetry and artwork to illustrate the importance and impact of being vulnerable with students; see Chapters 3–6 for examples.

During professional development sessions, we both explicitly model and then debrief instructional strategies, focusing on how teachers can adapt the process depending on their own students' needs. When introducing autobiographical poetry, for example, Alison first shared a series of templates for autobiographical poetry and a sample poem she wrote using images and languages from her own life, in this case, a template based on Lyon's iconic "Where I'm From" (1999); additional resources can be found at www.bravingup.com and at Teachers College Press at tcpress.com/dover-resources. Next, we modeled collaborative authorship as a scaffold toward independent writing; teachers then each wrote a line for the poem and shared them using the waterfall chat method described above. Alison cut and pasted the online chat into a Google Doc, and teachers worked together to decide how to order each line or phrase, which lines to combine, and which words (if any) to translate (see Figure 7.5).

Once the group agreed on a final structure for the poem, Alison guided teachers in analyzing how we used languaging when writing individual lines and assembling the poem. Key discussion points included the reasons why so many teachers wrote their own lines in English, and what teachers would do to affirm and model plurilingualism when teaching poetry in their own classrooms.

Following the session, teachers wrote complete poems of their own and developed strategies to scaffold students' plurilingual writing in their virtual classes. Language Explorer teachers Juan and Zineh, for example, developed plurilingual sentence frames in order to support students' development of poems about their social identities (Figure 7.6); these frames illustrate not only possible structures for a poem, but also how students might weave together multiple languages within and across stanzas. In presenting the frames to students, they invited students to think about when and how to use different parts of their linguistic repertoire by, for example,

Figure 7.5. Collaboratively Written Where I'm From Poem

Where We're From
Written by the Fall 2020
Language Explorer Teachers

I am from sweet tea and summer corn, from coffee in grandpa's Sunday
    morning kitchen
Soy de un hogar filled with smells and little balls of energy.
We are from chaos and laughter
I am from oceans and nước mắm (fish sauce)
From backyard bbq and grass filled yards
I am from a mountain of books and exotic fruit
I am from parents who are selfless, who sacrifice their own happiness
    for mine
I am rolling green hills and sticky skies
From soccer balls and spices
From a city of hope where the smell of a good coffee and football makes
    my Sunday.
We are from screen family gatherings [in a post-COVID world]
From warmth and good food
We are from blue waters and spicy salsa verde.
From where the Incas call home and maracuya
I am from the eagle with the serpent stained in red, white and green.
We are from there, and now we are here.

using language differently when presenting abstract versus concrete concepts, describing thoughts or feelings, or addressing different audiences.

Another Language Explorer teacher, Paola, opted to begin not with her own poetry, but with a series of activities exploring the relationship among specific words and phrases and the overarching meaning of a poem. She began by introducing the poetic form called "blackout poetry," which dates back to the 18th century but was popularized with the publication of Kleon's (2010) *Newspaper Blackout*. To write a blackout poem, a poet selects a page from an outside text, such as a novel or a newspaper, and then crosses out everything except a few words; the words that remain form the lyrics of a new poem.

Paola began by sharing the poem she and students would "black out," in this case, "What Is an Intersection?" (Browne, Acevedo, & Gatwood 2020). After reviewing a prior lesson about the concept of intersectionality (Crenshaw, 1989), Paola directed students to a Jamboard, where they

Figure 7.6. Using Plurilingual Sentence Frames When Writing Identity Poetry

You will write 2 stanzas para crear un poema with the entire class! Tienen que elegir 2 social identities to focus on.

STANZA #1 = Social Identity #1: an identity where you experience privilegio en tu comunidad
ESTROFA #2 = Social Identity #2: Identidad social that you are always consciente about (siempre piensas en este social identity)
Sentence Frame / Marco de Oración (Spanish and Inglés)

STANZA #1
LINE 1: Yo vivo en _____ (describe tu mundo)
LINE 2: Cómo _____ (describe tu social identity)
LINE 3 & 4: Dónde _____ (describe cómo sientes un privilegio with Social Identity #1)

ESTROFA #2
LINE 1: This is el mismo mundo donde _____ (mention social identity 2)
LINE 2: (¿Cuáles son los obstáculos que enfrentan debido al Social Identity 2?)
LINE 3: I wonder _____ (¿Qué parte de Social Identity #2 makes you worry?)
LINE 4: Me doy cuenta que I am _____

Identity Poem Template (created by Language Explorer Teachers Juan Pablo García and Zineh Abu Khalaf).

worked collaboratively to "black out" any words or ideas that did not reflect their own understanding of intersections. Students then analyzed the words that remained in order to develop a shared definition of intersectionality, focusing on how poets strategically use language to build meaning and increase the impact of their writing.

As the lesson progressed, students began to identify the words and concepts they wanted to explore in their own poetry. Once students selected the focus of their poems—in this case, what they would do if they could change the world—Paola adapted Viorst's (1984) poem "If I Were in Charge of the World" as a template for students. She then wrote her own plurilingual example (see Figure 7.7) and challenged students to use their full linguistic repertoire to voice their vision; examples of students' poems are featured after Chapters 1, 3, and 7 of this book.

Figure 7.7. Modeling Plurilingual Poetry

If I Were to Change the World . . .
(by Language Explorer Teacher Paola Rosenberg,
in the style of Viorst)

If I were to change the world,
I'd cancel the violence in the streets
I'd cancel el odio y el rencor
I'd even cancel student debt so an entire generation of people could
flourish financially

If I were in charge of the world,
There would be no judgements made against my skin which is bronzed by
the gods, but hated by many
There would be no more odio entre latinos criticando el color de nuestra
piel y abrazando nuestra cultura étnica centroamericana
There would even be celebration, support, and respect between all races,
where we acknowledge that underneath our skin we are all the same

If I were in charge of the world
You wouldn't have to put your name in a lottery to have access to an
excellent school
You wouldn't have to go to Tijuana para recibir tratamiento para sus
muelas
You wouldn't have to tener vergüenza de su acento en su lenguaje
materno ni en inglés porque eres un superhéroe con el poder de
plurilingüismo

If I were in charge of the world . . .
Kindness would be felt
Compassion would be heard
And Respect would be seen by las acciones de los ser humanos
Opiniones would still be allowed but not the actions of downcasting
others because they are not like you
If I were in charge of the world

By vulnerably sharing of themselves, scaffolding discussions, and modeling plurilingualism, teachers like Isaac, Juan, Zineh, and Paola are indeed rising to students' challenges to change the world.

Resources and Reflective Activities for Chapter 7

- Throughout this book, we have explored educators' approach to teaching in plurilingual classrooms, including how they embody each strand of translanguaging pedagogy (stance, design, and shift). When you think about your own practice before, during, and since the COVID-19 pandemic, how did each of these aspects of your teaching change or evolve?
- In this chapter, we examine how teachers can nourish culturally and linguistically sustaining online classrooms that embrace students' personal, cultural, and linguistic humanity. What supports and strategies did you use to humanize your own virtual classrooms? What worked? For whom? How do you know?
- What did you learn about your and your students' languaging as you moved from face-to-face to distance-based learning and back again? What kinds of obstacles and opportunities does this shift create?
- Examine your own online classroom and curricular resources; what languages, identities, and stories are most visible? How do you need to stretch in order to more fully represent your students and community?
- Select one of the scaffolds in this chapter and develop your own artifact to discuss with colleagues. What did you learn about each other when you shared this work? How could you adapt or integrate this scaffold into your own classroom?
- Additional resources related to plurilingual and humanizing online pedagogies can be found at www.bravingup.com and at Teachers College Press at tcpress.com/dover-resources.

If I Were to Change the World, by Mac Arjey Caisip

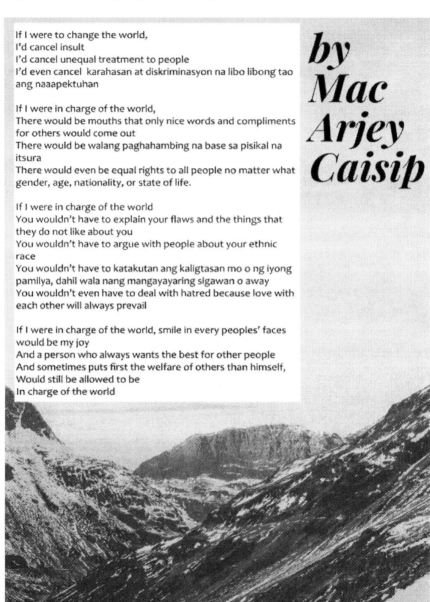

If I were to change the world,
I'd cancel insult
I'd cancel unequal treatment to people
I'd even cancel karahasan at diskriminasyon na libo libong tao
ang naaapektuhan

If I were in charge of the world,
There would be mouths that only nice words and compliments
for others would come out
There would be walang paghahambing na base sa pisikal na
itsura
There would even be equal rights to all people no matter what
gender, age, nationality, or state of life.

If I were in charge of the world
You wouldn't have to explain your flaws and the things that
they do not like about you
You wouldn't have to argue with people about your ethnic
race
You wouldn't have to katakutan ang kaligtasan mo o ng iyong
pamilya, dahil wala nang mangayayaring sigawan o away
You wouldn't even have to deal with hatred because love with
each other will always prevail

If I were in charge of the world, smile in every peoples' faces
would be my joy
And a person who always wants the best for other people
And sometimes puts first the welfare of others than himself,
Would still be allowed to be
In charge of the world

by
Mac
Arjey
Caisip

Part III

STRETCHING BEYOND
THE CLASSROOM

CHAPTER 8

Redefining Success: Comunidad, Confianza, and Complexity

In the previous chapters, we examined some of the ways educators can invite newcomer and emergent plurilingual students' voices into the classroom, use modeling and scaffolding to support their linguistic experimentation, and create opportunities for students to leverage their voices within and beyond the school walls. As program directors, we treasure the opportunity to watch each team of teachers take our annual curricular offering (a "skeleton," we call it) and bring it to life in a way we never imagined. As we argue throughout this book, braving up is not a set of tools or strategies, but rather a challenge to abandon the fallacy that education can or should be standardized for all learners, and an invitation to reconceptualize schooling as a culturally and linguistically sustaining experience. In this chapter, we explore some of the ways educators can brave up as we assess and evaluate the impact of our work, focusing on three critical markers of success: complexity, proficiency, and agency.

REDEFINING SUCCESS

One of the first questions we get about the Language Explorer program is invariably, "But does it work?" "Of course," we'd like to respond, "just look at this amazing poetry." Depending on the context, we suspect we'd be greeted with either a look of confusion and a reference to test scores, or a vibrant reflection about what we can learn when we authentically listen to our newcomer and emergent plurilingual students. Suffice to say, we prefer the latter! Nevertheless, we appreciate the imperative to evaluate how programmatic outcomes align with school and state learning targets; in Chapter 9, we examine this and other ways to support and sustain programs like the Language Explorer programs at the district level. Here, however, we wish to focus on a more comprehensive definition of success: how programs

like Language Explorers can affirm, engage, and amplify the assets of culturally, linguistically, and experientially diverse newcomer students.

For some teachers, as well as for many of our students, this represents
a significant departure from schooling-as-usual; teachers and students
alike have been socialized to see English proficiency, rather than multiliteracy, as the primary goal of language learning. As detailed in Chapter 2,
this approach is grounded in a monoglossic ideology and is characterized
by monolingual assessments that emphasize students' development of
"academic language" (which is interpreted as English-based disciplinary
vocabulary), and the valorization of an assimilationist, standardized voice
(Bernstein, 2020; Lopez, Turkan, & Guzman-Orth, 2017). Thus, braving up
requires us to find ways to support students' development of English proficiency while simultaneously stretching their overall linguistic repertoire
and affirming their identity as plurilingual beings. To do so, we must redefine concepts like "success," "achievement," and "academic learning" as
heteroglossic, co-constructed, and culturally and linguistically sustaining,
and strategically disrupt the false equivalence of assimilation and success.

As part of this process, we begin by inviting educators to consider what it
means to "succeed" as teachers of newcomer and emergent plurilingual students. During professional learning workshops, educators often respond with
ideas like "students leave with more confidence," "students feel empowered,"
"students develop their language," and "students explore their identities." We
wholeheartedly echo these responses, and we also recognize that these outcomes are both vague and incomplete. Newcomer and emergent plurilingual
students deserve educational experiences that are confidence-building, culturally and linguistically sustaining, and rigorous. Thus, we challenge teachers to operationalize their responses: What does an "A" in empowerment
actually look like? How will your students stretch their linguistic repertoire in
your classroom? What will change between the first and last day?

These questions are typically greeted with silence, followed by a flurry
of brainstorming. Figure 8.1 depicts one of the many rubrics developed by
Language Explorer teachers as they considered how to measure students'
growth over time. Teachers' use of the "sprouting-to-blooming" continuum
is based on the Community Forest activity described in Chapter 4, while the
emphasis on "bridging," "expanding," and "emerging" languaging reflects
the framing of the California English Language Development Standards
(California Department of Education, 2015).

This rubric illustrates one team of teachers' efforts to evaluate students' depth of exploration, reflection on their own multiple identities, and
strategic experimentation with language. However, there are still unan-
swered questions; how, for example, would you assess a poem like Ashley's

Figure 8.1. Measuring How Students Learn to Grow in Translanguaging Spaces

	In Full Bloom (4)	Blossoming (3)	Growing (2)	Sprouting (1)
Content	• Comprehensively explores multiple aspects of identity • Over the top detail • Vivid imagery	• Explores multiple aspects of identity • Includes many details • Creates an image in the reader's head	• Explores at least one aspect of identity • Includes some detail and imagery	• Limited exploration of identity • Few or no details • Limited imagery
Languaging	• Powerful voice • Creative, effective and varied vocabulary • Full use of linguistic repertoire	• Student's voice is clearly heard • Wide array of words used • Bridging linguistic repertoire	• Student's voice is emerging • Some variety in word choice • Expanding use of linguistic repertoire	• Hard to hear student's voice • Limited linguistic variety • Emerging use of linguistic repertoire

Teacher-created rubric for assessing student writing.

(included in Chapter 4), which is written entirely in English and includes few examples of figurative language but is rich in its interrogation of identity? Or Jamal's split-image portrait (included in Chapter 5), Steven's autobiographical comic (Chapter 5), or the first and final drafts of Lucha's autobiography (Chapter 6)?

These are the kinds of questions we routinely pose as part of our professional learning and coaching sessions for Language Explorer teachers, where we examine the many ways teachers can use rubrics like this one: for pre- and post-assessments of student work, to compare our expectations to those of our colleagues, and as tools for students' self-assessment and revision. One year we used rubrics to evaluate our efficacy as educators; teachers looked at an entire set of student projects, scored themselves based on trends in student performance, and planned for next steps in the classroom. Additional examples of professional learning and reflection protocols are available at www.bravingup .com and at Teachers College Press at tcpress.com/dover-resources.

What we *do not do*, however, is use rubrics to assign "grades" to our Language Explorer students, who are already subjected to far too many external labels. Instead, we frame assessment as a tool for growth, not a mechanism through which we assign value to students or encourage linguistic assimilation.

In the pages that follow, we model our assessment process by analyzing examples of student work and evaluating what success can look like when we brave up. Throughout, we center on three primary processes: (1) students' linguistic experimentation and syntactic complexity, (2) educators' professional growth as teachers of newcomer and emergent plurilingual students, and (3) enactments of agency within and beyond the classroom.

EXPERIMENTING WITH LANGUAGING AND
SYNTACTIC COMPLEXITY

Linguistic comfort refers to students' increasing willingness to draw upon their full linguistic repertoire and experiment with diverse languaging practices (Wubs-Mrozewicz, 2020). During the first few days of any Language Explorer program, students are often reluctant to pull from their full linguistic repertoires. During an introductory reflection, for example, teacher Nadia (who is not a fluent Spanish speaker) noted that

> My Spanish speaking students seemed to feel uncomfortable speaking
> Spanish around me at first. . . . Ella (my Russian speaker) would
> only use English and relied heavily on Google Translate. I have been
> encouraging my students (especially Ella and Rico due to their very

limited English) to use their primary language whenever they feel more comfortable.

As Nadia built relationships with students, she explicitly and intentionally encouraged students to experiment with and extend their emergent plurilingualism by stretching her own linguistic repertoire: "I decided to just use as much language as I knew to show by example that it is okay to not be able to say things 100% correctly because it is a safe space." As detailed in Chapters 4 through 7, this type of vulnerability enables educators to create a linguistically "brave space" (Arao & Clemens, 2013; Dover & Rodríguez-Valls, 2018), where students are willing to challenge themselves as thinkers, speakers, writers, and communicators. Moreover, by continually assessing students' shifting languaging practices and evolving metalinguistic awareness, teachers can focus on expanding the syntactic complexity of students' thinking and writing.

Bulté and Housen (2012, p. 22) summarize research on syntactic complexity as consisting of the following three core ideas: (a) the "use of more challenging and difficult language . . . [as] learners produce elaborated

Figure 8.2. Alondra

Alondra's complete response on Day 1:

My name is [Alondra], i am from India, i born in India And in 2017 i came to us and i was'nt know any english i join 8th grade and i learned English and i try my best of my ability and i did it, in ELD i get award for great achievement in english. USA is different than India

Excerpt of Alondra's response on Day 16 (she wrote 1 page):

My name is [Alondra], I am 14 years old. I borned in India, I am from India. In India I lived with my family and when I was 12 years old I moved to USA. I was sad because I left my family and friends. In USA when I started my eight grade i was exited but also nervous because I didn't know english. My first day at school was so nice I met new people at school they were so nice they helped me for everything, also helped me learn english. I am so lucky to have friends. I tried my best of my ability to learn English and I did it . . . after my eight grade my summer vacation got start. In summer I hangout with my friend enjoy with my friend and after summer vacation my high school started. . . . School wasn't easy as much as I was thinking. I am still in ELD that's why it was little hard for me . . .

Figure 8.3. Lazaro

Excerpt of Lazaro's response on Day 1 (he wrote 1 page):

> My name is [Lazaro]. I'm from Vietnam. Now, I lived in the United States of American. I lived with my family. I'm grade 12 . . . I don't have more friend, actually I just have 2 or 3 friends . . . When I came to American, the first person help me is "Chau", she is a senior, no she is graduated . . . I just want to say "thank you" to her . . . Next I want to introduce my dream . . . I know all most people in the world have a dream, me too. I want to become a lawyer because I wish I can help people stand on the side of justice . . . I always help people when I can help . . . I don't want to have a war in the world . . .

Excerpt of Lazaro's response on Day 16 (he wrote 2 pages)

> I study Elementary and middle school in Vietnam . . . I stud high school one year in Vietnam, I need to move go to the United States . . . I am happy because I have a new life . . . I learn a lot of thing . . . I impressive them so much . . . I wonder why people helped me so much . . . Summer Language Academy helped me to find my mind help me know "who I am" help me know what need to do for my future . . . I love music I can play ukulele, organ and piano. I want to learn all the musical. I want to discover . . . I know I can't go around the world but I need to go half world. It sounds a bit crazy right? LOL . . . I love the world.

language" (Ellis & Barkhuizen, 2005, p. 139); (b) the use of a "wide variety of both basic and sophisticated structures and words" (Wolf-Quintero, Inagaki, & Kim, 1998, p. 69); and (c) the "complexity of the underlying interlanguage system developed" and used by student writers (Skehan, 2003, p. 8). Consider, for example, the following pre- and post-assessments of student writing, which depict how emergent plurilingual students responded to our invitation to "tell us who you are" on the first and last day of their 16-day summer Language Explorer program. Note that teachers didn't comment on or return students' pre-assessments; thus, students' post-assessments reflect the evolution of their thinking and languaging in response to this prompt, rather than a "revision" of their initial draft.

In each of these excerpts, we see students demonstrating an increasing use of complex syntax and vocabulary, a wider variety of phrases and structures, and a willingness to stretch their linguistic repertoire (for example, when Lazaro says he "impressive them so much" or Davinci refers to his

Figure 8.4. Davinci

Excerpt of Davinci's response on Day 1 (he wrote 3 sentences)

> I can interpretes si esta escrito pero mejor leyendo y saber lo que hice pero hablarlo todavía no puedo pronunciarlo bien I don't like write because me equivocare y me tardo mas escribirlo que leerlo . . .

Excerpt of Davinci's response on Day 16 (he wrote 1 page)

> Cuando yo estaba pequeño me costaba comprender . . . ingles se me hacia difícil pero con lo que he aprendido y me han ensenado no están impossible como lo que yo pensaba la forma tan amigable de como me ensenan perder el miedo a poder hablarlo . . . me gusta mucho aprender cosas nuevas sobre el idioma . . . y me gusta el sentido del humor para saber las cosas . . . como el árbol lleva surface, shallow y deep culture . . . aprender sobre diferentes culturas idiomas que si podemos lograr lo que se nos hacia difícil de aprender[13]

learning about "surface, shallow y deep culture"). As educators, we can look at writings like these through multiple lenses—narrowly through the lens of "correctness," or more broadly as we consider what they reveal about the process of braving up: when we build community/*comunidad* in the classroom, we support emergent plurilingual students in having the confidence/*confianza* to grow.

COMUNIDAD, CONFIANZA, AND COMPLEXITY

In the pages that follow, we examine what students' writing reveals about the interrelationship among three key concepts: community/*comunidad*, confidence/*confianza*, and complexity. In so doing, we are presenting a model that is shaped by our own cultural identities and plurilingual repertories; constructs like "community" and "confidence" emerge differently in English and Spanish, and this model illustrates the cognitive potentialities that emerge when we interweave, rather than separate, multiple named languages. In Spanish, for example, *comunidad* emphasizes the idea of collective effort and understanding; in the classroom, this might manifest in the form of emphases on *pertenencia* (belonging), *búsqueda* (searching), and *participativa* (participating). Similarly, incorporating the idea of *confianza* into our understanding of confidence centers the reciprocal relationships necessary to create affirming, brave spaces. We encourage readers to consider how they might engage their—and their students'—full linguistic repertoires when building conceptual models like this one; when educators and students co-construct meaning, the results are invariably more creative, complex, and comprehensive than anything adults could have developed alone.

Building Community/*Comunidad*

In reflecting on her experience in a Language Explorer classroom, teacher Josefa commented that

> The best day of the program was the last day; the students were engaged in a community art project, making a wall-sized poster as a class, and the conversations were happening across languages. Students were comparing words in Portuguese and Spanish. Students were teaching and learning words in Chinese. Students were sharing their stories with their peers and teachers in a way they hadn't before. It was a moving experience, and it could not have happened if the students had not been given the time and space to engage in their culture.

Throughout this book, we have explored some of the ways educators can create heteroglossic classrooms that invite and affirm newcomer and emergent plurilingual students' voices. In this quote, as well as in the student writing samples above, we see the impact of these efforts. Just as Josefa reflects upon the organic emergence of a multilingual cacophony, so too do students highlight their own journey from isolation toward community.

Like many newcomer students (such as Paolo, who you met in Chapter 6), Alondra's first months in the United States were marked by loneliness and difficulties building friendships. However, as she built relationships within the Language Explorer classroom, she learned to rely on the emotional support of her peers; this enabled her to push herself linguistically and academically, within and beyond the Language Explorer walls. For Lazaro, who entered our classroom with a more fully developed social network at school, the program provided an opportunity to consider what he brings to his relationships: "I wonder why people helped me so much . . . Summer Language Academy helped me to find my mind [and] help me know 'who I am.'" As students become more confident that they will be welcomed and affirmed within and beyond the classroom, they develop the confidence to stretch as learners—and to begin to demand that schools respond to their unique interests and needs.

Leveraging Confidence/*Confianza*

When educators nourish brave, heteroglossic classrooms, newcomer and emergent plurilingual students rise to the challenge. On a daily basis, we see students stretching their linguistic repertoires by experimenting with languaging in English, while simultaneously deepening their use of their additional languages. This is evident in Davinci's narrative, as he both reflects on his initial fears of writing ("I do not want to write because I will do it wrong") and later notes that he has realized that "nothing is impossible like I thought," saying that teachers "taught me in a friendly way."

In monoglossic classrooms, plurilingual students are forced into daily confrontations with explicit and implicit actions that position monolingualism as the norm (Flores & Rosa, 2015). However, when teachers embrace and amplify students' cultural and linguistic identities, we create opportunities for students like Davinci to challenge deficit-based language practices that silence, shame, and marginalize their voices. Rather than learning to silence himself to avoid doing it "wrong," Davinci is beginning to think of language as something that can be interesting, friendly, and explored with humor.

Scaffolding Complexity

When Brenda entered our classroom as a 10th-grader, she had been enrolled in U.S. schools for 3 years but was not making progress in the context of her district's English Language Development courses; state assessments identified her as "minimally developed" in her oral and written skills in English. Like Alondra, Lazaro, and Davinci, Brenda's pre- and post-assessments provide insight into her experience as a newcomer and emergent plurilingual student, as well as how braving up enabled her to reach new levels of syntactic and conceptual complexity. Figure 8.5 features Brenda's narrative on the 1st and 16th day of the program, and it includes examples of how we might annotate student writing for the purposes of professional learning.

Brenda's first response emphasized superficial aspects of identity, such as favorite colors and foods; she also indicated her life goals of becoming famous. As Brenda became more comfortable within the classroom community/*comunidad*, she developed the confidence/*confianza* to share more of herself by reflecting on her relationships with members of her family and considering how they have informed—and been informed by—her migration experiences. She also offers insight into her dream of becoming an astronaut and how that dream was encouraged and inspired by her parents. She closes her narrative with an expression of optimism and confidence, one that can both propel her into her future and help educators know how to encourage and support her socially and academically.

Figure 8.5. Brenda

Brenda's full response on Day 1:

My name is [Brenda] I from acapulco gerrero. I have 15 year old and my mom nme is [Luce] and dad names is [Rico] they anbos from acapulco. My favorite food it sushy and my favorite plais to go it san Francisco and beach and my favorite animals it my dog mallo I take my time with hem it the only one understand on my problem and my favorite color it green and black and I want a make my dream come true a want to be famous like liza Koshy my favorite sport it lucha Romana and my favorite fruit it durasno I born here 4 year. I want to bisitar difrent Plais like francia, Italia, El Salvador, and another I want to prube diferent food to tray another thigs I don want to be merry yet and I love my family fin.

Superficial aspects of identity

Increasing confidence, cognitive and syntactic complexity

Brenda's full response on Day 16:

Hi my name it [Brenda] I have 15 year old and I from acapulco gerero and this its tock ebriting about I come to U.S.A. to have a different life and to have a god future. When I was a little grll I always say to my dad I want to be a stranaut doctor or another things in that time was funny because the only thing my dad sed it you can do ebrithing you want but you have to be a great student in school. I was 5 year with my dad then I moving to Tijuana I was 7 years with my tios my life in Tijuana was bad I was thinking to go back to acapulco with my dad and to know my new my sister itza then I tell my dad to go back to acapulco and he sed yes I wasso happy and move quiet because ((dejare el pasado atras)) then the years will pass my mom call me and she tell me to go to U.S.A. and have a good life and I sed yes. When I lif I was cray [cry] and hugging my sister she wen know what happen if I tell her she probable cray then I and my dad had a long trip and when we arrived at our destination I said goodbye to him and took different direction and now I have a life to differentiate and I know I will fulfill my dreams and se my family agan.

Deeper aspects of identity

Use of parentheses indicate metalinguistic awareness

By creating an environment where students like Brenda are empowered to write freely, educators develop a more complete understanding of emergent plurilingual students' use of language. Moreover, by encouraging Brenda to translanguage, teachers were able to see, for example, how her use of phonetic spelling in Spanish ("b" for "v" as she writes "bisitar" rather than "visitar") carries over into English ("ebrithing" for "everything"); they could then plan instruction to scaffold Brenda's specific linguistic needs and support her progress toward fluency. Thus, rather than labeling Brenda as "minimally developed," Brenda's teachers were able to track and scaffold her increasing syntactic complexity and metalinguistic awareness, as she used increasingly sophisticated phrases to represent the passage of time ("I always say," "I was thinking"), evolution of identity (". . . took different direction and now I have a life"), and metacognition about languaging (such as her parenthetical use of "((dejare el pasado atras))").

DEVELOPING HETEROGLOSSIC PROFICIENCY

In addition to looking for evidence of students' willingness to explore their identities and experiment with complex linguistic registers, variances, and nuances, we also ask teachers to reflect on their own evolving professional and cultural proficiency as teachers of newcomer and emergent plurilingual students (see Chapter 1). In Chapters 2 and 3, we explore the imperative for teachers to challenge monoglossic ideologies that equate "success" with the erasure of students' cultural and linguistic identities, resulting in a form of "social death" (Cacho, 2012) as students are forced to navigate educational institutions that work "against participants' enactment of self . . . and work toward devaluing their lives" (Rodriguez, 2020, p. 3).

Creating a linguistically inclusive classroom calls for the strategic and intentional design of activities, assessments, and scaffolds that challenge monoglossia and empower language learners to leverage their full linguistic repertoires (Martin-Beltrán, 2014). For many educators—and some students—accomplishing this goal requires a significant disruption of schooling-as-usual. Students have been socialized to see English proficiency as the primary goal of their educational experience, and educators to interpret fluency in the locally dominant languages as normal, natural, and desirable (see Ek, Sánchez, & Quijada Cerecer, 2013, for more); within the context of our work in Southern California, this can result in a diglossic overreliance on languages of colonization, namely English and Spanish, or hierarchical models of "correct" and "incorrect" linguistic registers.

However, as we discuss in Chapter 2, when educators brave up and stretch their own linguistic repertoires, they become willing to face their own linguistic insecurities and stretch beyond their own zones of language comfort. In so doing, they move from a position of linguistic fragility[14] to one of unlimited potential and strength.

EMPOWERMENT AND AGENCY

At the beginning of each year of the Language Explorers, we invite teachers to reflect on their own questions, strengths, and areas for growth regarding their work with emergent plurilingual students. Over the course of the program, we challenge them to share vignettes and student work samples that illustrate their struggles and successes. This isn't always easy for teachers, many of whom have been conditioned to think of self-assessment as more perfunctory (as in the case of mandated performance assessments and scheduled evaluations) than productive. It is uncomfortable to admit that we are struggling to connect with a specific student or share a video clip from a lesson where we did more talking than listening, and sometimes even more so to "boast" about a classroom success. Braving up, however, requires us to vulnerably share ourselves with our students and colleagues, as we leverage our strengths, learn from our missteps, and creatively disrupt normative educational processes.

In Chapter 6, we examined some of the ways educators can support newcomer and emergent plurilingual students in coming to believe that they are entitled to an educational experience that affirms their personal, cultural, and linguistic identities, as well as encouraging them to experiment with ways to use their voices to effect change. We consider this enactment of agency among the most important markers of success, as it represents a fundamental shift in ownership over educational processes. As we as educators co-construct learning activities with newcomer students, co-define what "exemplary" work means and represents, and disrupt our own professional and linguistic dominance, we begin to position emergent plurilingual students as critical actors within their schools and communities.

It is not uncommon for teachers to describe their work with the Language Explorer programs as "transformative" for both students and themselves. To quote teacher Lupe:

> I have worked for [this district] for almost 30 years, there is no other program or class that empowers the students to be themselves as [much as the Language Explorers]. It equips them at the most critical and vulnerable time in their lives. It gives them the right to be themselves as they merge in the vast current of the new culture and language.

When Lupe talks about the Language Explorer programs as empowering, equipping, and giving students the "right to be themselves," she is implicitly critiquing her 30 years of experience with schooling that disempowers, disrupts, and silences plurilingual students. This represents a tremendous shift; when educators define their own success not as *supporting* emergent plurilingual students, but as *empowering* them, they experience the imperative to promote change.

For teachers like Liana, a veteran educator who described herself as having little experience working with newcomers prior to the Language Explorer program, this imperative to promote change is a critical first step:

Working with such a different group of students has opened my eyes to look beyond the surface. I don't think I will ever teach the same way, I will make an effort to connect with my students and really get to know them. Sure, we get to know our students during the school year but this program has shown me that there's always so much more that isn't shared. Understanding my students' stories will help me be a better educator and have a larger impact on their life.

We love that working with our students was an inspirational experience for Liana, and we have witnessed the ways she continues to brave up in the classroom. However, in a state like California, where 40% of public school students are plurilingual, and almost 18% of students are identified as emergent speakers of English (CDE, 2021a), it is implausible that the Language Explorer program was Liana's first encounter with newcomer and emergent plurilingual students. Instead, her comments point to the structural invisibility of newcomer and emergent plurilingual students within the context of her day-to-day experiences as a teacher. Essentially, Liana didn't see her students, and thus neither learned about nor taught toward them.

In Chapter 9, which we co-authored with Dr. Renae Bryant, one of our district partners and a visionary advocate for emergent plurilingual students, we move beyond the classroom to examine how students, families, educators, and district administrators can use their collective agency to nourish and sustain radically inclusive schooling at the local, district, and state levels. Throughout, we focus on the imperative to (a) learn from our students before we teach them, (b) challenge monoglossic and hierarchical policies, and (c) build coalitions that reflect and amplify the strengths, values, and priorities of newcomer students and communities.

Resources and Reflective Activities for Chapter 8

- In this chapter, we present a plurilingual model that illustrates how our own cultural identities and linguistic repertoires shape our understanding of educational processes (in this case, the nuances of community/ *comunidad* and confidence/*confianza*). How do you draw on your and your students' plurilingual repertoires when constructing meaning in your own classroom?
- In this chapter, we explore multiple ways we might define success, focusing on success in terms of complexity, proficiency, and agency. How does this framework reflect your own approach to evaluating your—and students'—success?

- As you read Alondra, Lazaro, Davinci, and Brenda's writing, what did you notice? If these were your students, what would you do to support and challenge them as they continue to brave up?
- This chapter featured a different genre of student writing than the examples elsewhere in this book (i.e., the student poetry included after Chapters 1, 3, and 7). What did you notice about the ways students used language differently as they wrote for different purposes and audiences?
- Additional resources for professional learning can be found at www .bravingup.com and at Teachers College Press at tcpress.com/dover-resources; these include more comprehensive analyses of Alondra, Lazaro, and Davinci's writing; self-assessment rubrics; and reflection protocols.

CHAPTER 9

Blossoming From Roots to Trees

Supporting, Sustaining, and Advocating for Radically Inclusive Teaching

with Renae Bryant, Anaheim Union High School District

Throughout this book, we have explored ideological, curricular, and pedagogical aspects of braving up, focusing on the tremendous opportunities that emerge when educators engage and affirm the identities, voices, and experiences of newcomer and emergent plurilingual students. In this final chapter, we take a wider lens as we consider the systemic factors that enable programs like the Language Explorers to thrive, examining ways to initiate, support, and sustain radically inclusive approaches at the local, district, and state levels.

Over the past decade, we have worked with school districts throughout California to create, refine, and evaluate a wide array of programs for migrant, immigrant, newcomer, and emergent plurilingual students; collectively, these programs have engaged hundreds of educators and thousands of students. Each of these partnerships is unique, reflecting the situated cultural, linguistic, and sociopolitical identities of the school and community. As we emphasize throughout this book, the Language Explorer programs are far from standardized, and we draw inspiration and insight from each new team of educators and students. However, the most successful Language Explorer programs—those that are truly transformative for students and educators alike—have several key characteristics in common: they (a) position newcomer and emergent plurilingual students as partners within—not objects of—educational processes; (b) encourage innovation among teachers and key personnel; and (c) strategically leverage fiscal, political, and institutional resources in order to generate support for cultural and linguistically sustaining practices.

In this chapter, which is co-authored with Dr. Renae Bryant, a leader in one of our partner school districts, we examine ways to position programs like Language Explorers for sustainability and success. Throughout, we draw examples from Renae's own school district, as well as the many other districts with whom we have worked.

KNOW YOUR CONTEXT

Located in Southern California, Anaheim Union High School District (AUHSD) enrolls approximately 30,000 students across 20 middle and high school campuses, and it employs more than 1,200 teachers. Twenty percent of AUHSD's students are emergent plurilinguals, and with 54 languages spoken within the district, it is among the most linguistically diverse school districts in California. AUHSD has a large community of newcomer students and families, welcoming approximately 300 newcomer students from over 20 different countries each year.

Renae joined AUHSD in 2017 as the district's director of English Learner and Multilingual Services. A former elementary and secondary school teacher leader, Renae was already widely recognized for her leadership in multilingual education: she had been named bilingual Teacher of the Year at the district, county, and state levels, and she coordinated and directed multilingual programming in school districts throughout Southern California. As is the case for the many teachers and administrators who champion Language Explorer programs, for Renae, working with newcomer and emergent plurilingual students is not a "job responsibility" but an imperative; when a district doesn't serve newcomer and emergent plurilingual students, it doesn't serve students.

Renae was drawn to AUHSD for its emphasis on community partnerships, multilingual education, civic engagement, and innovation. It was the first district in its county to offer the California State Seal of Biliteracy on students' diplomas, an award given to students who demonstrate their multilingual fluency in English and another language. In 2021, a total of 1,303 Seal of Biliteracy Awards were earned in American Sign Language, Arabic, Bengali, Chinese, French, Indonesian, Japanese, Korean, Mandarin, Tagalog, and Vietnamese. In 2020, almost 1,100 AUHSD students earned this recognition; of these students, 77% had formerly been designated as "English Learners" (CDE, 2021b). At the time of Renae's hire, AUHSD had completed its second Summer Language Academy (in 2016) and was emerging as a local and national model for its innovative, wraparound approach to building academically and newcomer and emergent plurilingual students and communities. In the years since, AUHSD's Language Explorer programs have received multiple awards, including the 2018 Cultural and Linguistic

Responsiveness Award from the Orange County Department of Education and the 2019 California School Board Association's Golden Bell Award for programmatic excellence. The district regularly hosts tours for educational leaders interested in developing programs for newcomers and has come to function as an informal learning laboratory for preservice and early-career educators interested in learning about newcomer communities and plurilingual pedagogies.

There is much that makes AUHSD unique, from the cultural and linguistic diversity of its student body to the visionary leadership of its superintendent and school board. AUHSD Superintendent Michael Matsuda is himself the child of Japanese-Americans who were forced out of an Anaheim high school and into an internment camp during World War II (Mitchell, 2016). He never learned his heritage language of Japanese and speaks openly about how his experiences with racism and linguistic oppression fuel his passion for multilingual education, civic engagement, and educational equity and justice.

Prior to becoming superintendent, Michael taught for 22 years in AUHSD and he now uses his position to not only center but amplify the voices of, the district's most marginalized students; he expects each of the district's 3,000 employees to do the same. He is unwavering in his commitment to academic excellence and challenges AUHSD's students to leverage their voices at the local, state, and national levels.

> "Do you work for education or does education work for you?"
> —Superintendent Michael Matsuda's question to the 30,000 students
> Anaheim Union High School District (AUHSD) serves.

In a recent op-ed about the importance of student activism as an expression of democracy, for example, Michael describes the many ways in which AUHSD's students can be labeled, noting that

> . . . almost 20 percent of our young people are homeless. Many are sleeping on floors, in motels, or on the streets. They are exposed to all kinds of trauma. They are food-deprived, isolated, depressed, and, like many of their peers, anxious about their future and the uncertain economy. (Matsuda, 2020)

However, rather than seeing these labels as indicative of the district's "needs," Michael focuses on how those experiences contribute to students' unique insights, perspectives, and opportunity to impact American democracy. AUHSD's student body, says Michael

. . . is also highly engaged and activated when it comes to civic learning and participation. . . .they speak up on the issues that matter to them, including teen suicide, depression, human trafficking, housing, bias, access to clean air and water, immigration, and global warming, among others. They write to their elected officials and appear at school board and city council meetings. . . . They plant trees, serve food to the homeless, work in school gardens, teach seniors to use social media, write troops overseas, and make toys for sheltered animals. (Matsuda, 2020)

In AUHSD, the Language Explorer programs both emerged from and embody a districtwide commitment to educational equity, student voice, and civic action (see Figure 9.1). This is true for many, but not all, of the districts with whom we have worked. In the following section we explore the process through which we begin conversations in districts with less experience engaging in radically inclusive education.

FIND COMMON GROUND

In 1980, legal scholar Derrick Bell coined the term *interest convergence* as a way of understanding how and why the civil rights of minoritized groups— in this case Black communities impacted by school segregation prior to the 1954 *Brown v. Board of Education* decision—become prioritized within

Figure 9.1. AUHSD Core Values

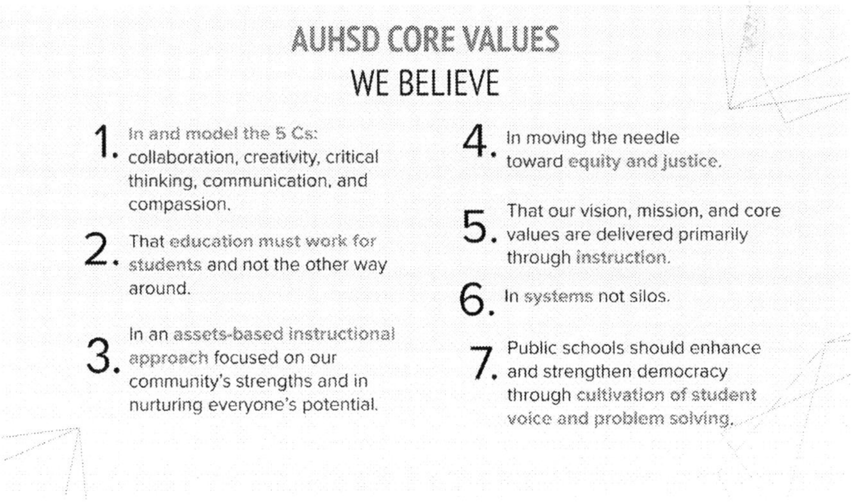

AUHSD CORE VALUES
WE BELIEVE

1. In and model the 5 Cs: collaboration, creativity, critical thinking, communication, and compassion.

2. That education must work for students and not the other way around.

3. In an assets-based instructional approach focused on our community's strengths and in nurturing everyone's potential.

4. In moving the needle toward equity and justice.

5. That our vision, mission, and core values are delivered primarily through instruction.

6. In systems not silos.

7. Public schools should enhance and strengthen democracy through cultivation of student voice and problem solving.

institutional systems. Bell argues that it is *only* when the interests of privileged groups (i.e., White communities) converge with those of minoritized communities that change occurs (such as the end of de jure segregation). While the concept of interest convergence often carries a negative connotation for its emphasis on the self-serving motives that fuel some institutional responses to oppression, we find it an extremely valuable entry point through which to initiate systemic change.

Virtually all of the teachers and educational leaders who approach us about starting a Language Explorer program are passionate advocates for newcomer and emergent plurilingual students. They may have heard about our work from students or colleagues, toured a Language Explorer classroom in another district, or seen a media report about one of our programs. They are enthusiastic about creating a brave space within their own district, one in which students and educators can explore languaging, identity, and culture as they develop a shared foundation for academic success. Sometimes there is already districtwide buy-in for a Language Explorer program; other times, they draw a contrast between the culture of their school district and our existing partners: "It's not like that here," they might say. "We'll have to fly under the radar." By that, they typically mean that there are members of the community who operate from a deficit perspective when working with newcomer and emergent plurilingual students and who want to emphasize remediation or establishing basic skills in English (i.e., monoglossic practices that reinforce Standard English as the most important and appropriate register). Other times, a district will tell us they "only want to do part of it," and ask if we can deliver a prepackaged curriculum for their teachers to implement. These requests are typically accompanied by an apologetic admission that the schedule or budget doesn't allow time for teacher recruitment, training, reflection, or debriefing.

We have learned to work intentionally and strategically in cases like these. As we discuss throughout this book, braving up is not about adopting quick-fix "tools" or "strategies," but an ideological shift from an educational approach that stigmatizes, standardizes, and regulates emergent plurilingual students' languaging to one that positions them as important and influential members of the educational community. This type of transformation requires a systemic commitment to equity, the institutional leadership necessary to overcome resistance, and the willingness to allocate resources—including time, people, and money—in the interests of newcomer and emergent plurilingual students.

Thus, instead of agreeing to implement a "stand-alone" Language Explorer program—or, as we were recently asked, one in which we bury the Language Explorer curriculum within a 6-hour computerized "basic skills" program—we instead ask prospective partners to talk to us about their district and its priorities. Why are they interested in a new approach to working with newcomer and emergent plurilingual students? What academic, ideological, political, or community "problem" is the district hoping to solve? What are the district's greatest strengths and institutional values? How are newcomer and emergent plurilingual communities currently involved in school processes? As we learn who the district is, and who it wants to be, we are able to support district leadership in developing a plan that, in the words of educational scholar H. Richard Milner IV, challenges people to "start where you are, but don't stay there" (2020).

ENGAGE KEY STAKEHOLDERS

AUHSD's first Summer Language Academy developed in response to a significant cultural and linguistic shift within the district's newcomer communities (see the sidebar, "Never Waste a Crisis"). As a district with strong internal leadership and a history of robust and reciprocal relationships with diverse community stakeholders, they were able to establish a Newcomer Task Force and implement its recommendations fairly quickly. Moreover, by strategically recruiting task force members who were connected to other districtwide initiatives, they established a foundation for institutionalizing systemic change.

Never Waste a Crisis

Every success begins with a sense of urgency and a deeper "why." For AUHSD's Language Explorer programs, this came in 2015, when school districts across California welcomed an influx of newcomers, many of whom were refugees, from the Middle East. This group of students was culturally, linguistically, and experientially unique within the district's newcomer communities, and this created both an opportunity and a challenge for the district. In response, AUHSD established a Newcomers Task Force so that diverse community stakeholders, including teachers, administrators, community leaders, parents, and counselors, could think collectively about how to best engage these new students. Ultimately, the task force advocated for a "summer bridge" experience to help newcomers acclimate to the district, build community, and establish a foundation for academic success. They brought their recommendation to the school board, and this led to the district's first Summer Language Academy and its emphasis on identity, languaging, and relationship-building.

(continued)

Questions for Reflection: What are your district's values, vision, and mission? How are they related specifically to newcomers and emerging plurilingual students? What is your district's "why," and how can it be leveraged to build programs for newcomer and emergent plurilingual scholars?

In many districts, however, newcomer and emergent plurilingual communities have been invisible, silent, or absent during conversations about district processes, and the first step is simply getting to know one another. Alison will never forget attending a meeting during which an elementary school principal was presenting data regarding test scores at her school site. "We're happy with how the students are progressing," she said, "except for a few subgroups." By this she meant students identified as English Learners or students with Individualized Education Programs (IEPs). However, when asked what languages were spoken by the 22 emergent plurilingual students at the school, the principal responded that she "couldn't be expected to know things like that off the top of her head," but said that the school was doing its part by hosting monthly pizza dinners for "those families." Unsurprisingly, those dinners were poorly attended. When leaders do not know and value their students, they cannot possibly engage them as partners in educational transformation.

In our experience, virtually every school site has faculty known for building especially robust relationships with their newcomer and emergent plurilingual students. We encourage districts to identify and include these "champions" as part of their Language Explorer leadership team; they will prove invaluable in developing programming that is locally achievable, high-yield, and authentically grounded in the strengths, values, and priorities of newcomer students and communities. Other members to consider include supportive administrators, university and community partners, parents, and newcomer students themselves; each will bring unique insight and creative suggestions regarding programmatic offerings. Refer to Chapter 6 for examples of how one of our partner districts invites emergent plurilingual students to participate in establishing district-level priorities.

It Takes a Village

AUHSD has an instructional vision and guiding principles that serve as a compass for its efforts to increase equity, access, and opportunity for emergent plurilingual students (see Figure 9.1). As its work with the Newcomer

Task Force evolved, district leaders worked strategically to consider how the newcomer programming fit within the district's overarching vision and structure. They developed a districtwide English Learner Task Force (with the help of a statewide advocacy network, Californians Together, http://www.californianstogether.org) and established priorities related to listening, speaking, reading, and writing; integrated and designated ELD; monitoring; and parent conferencing. They also created a Career Preparedness Systems Framework that emphasizes hard skills (technical skills), 21st-century skills (soft skills), and student voice and purpose (see McCrea, 2021, for more on this framework); this is used by all students (not only emergent plurilingual students) and is one of the ways the district works toward rigor and alignment among seemingly disparate groups of scholars in the district.

Next, AUHSD created EL Task Force Teams at each school site. These teams help leaders identify and track their progress in working with emergent plurilingual students generally, and newcomer students specifically, at each unique school site. The district EL Task Force meets monthly, and district leaders meet individually with each site team twice annually. This helps the district identify common and site-specific strengths and opportunities. Through this process, the district learned that for many of the newcomer students who entered our district midyear, summer was too long to wait for a dedicated Language Explorer program. This led to the expansion of academic year programs for newcomer students, including the development of twice-monthly Saturday Language Academies and school-university partnerships focusing on additional professional learning for subject area teachers.

Questions for reflection: How can you build on the work you are already doing for multilingual scholars? What is the next step in your effort? Who are your partners as you identify better and more cohesive ways to serve your district's diverse community of multilingual scholars?

ESTABLISH A PROGRAMMATIC IDENTITY
AND BUILD CAPACITY

In addition to serving as an advisory board, strategically selected stakeholder teams can also help districts brainstorm creative ways to engage, learn from, and build capacity among diverse members of the school community. In AUHSD, for example, the district partnered with school sites and community groups to establish districtwide and site-specific priorities; this both prevented the siloing of newcomer programs and maximized opportunities for innovation. Moreover, by focusing simultaneously on both district- and site-level analyses, it became apparent that while some teachers and administrators were fluent in the experiences of emergent plurilingual and newcomer students, others rarely interacted with the district's newcomers. Similarly, though many educators had expertise in the teaching of emergent plurilingual students, others had limited training, fear about promoting inclusive languaging in the classroom, or overt monoglossic ideologies.

This is not an uncommon phenomenon. School systems are large and multifaceted, and they are likely to employ educators with tremendous professional, cultural, linguistic, and ideological diversity. Moreover, newcomer and emergent plurilingual students sometimes exist at the margins of a school community; as newcomers, they rarely have prior relationships with teachers or school personnel; may not be in positions of student leadership; and are often concentrated in classes taught by a subgroup of teachers (i.e., those who teach courses designated for emergent plurilingual students). This can result in widespread ignorance and misunderstanding about the identities and experiences of newcomer students. In many cases, educators—including teachers, administrators, school, and district personnel—do not understand the differences among diverse groups of (im)migrant and language learning students, resulting in an inability to provide academically, culturally, or linguistically appropriate instruction.

As we detail in Chapter 3, professional learning and experiential pedagogy are critically important elements of our efforts to transform education. In many of our Language Explorer programs, teachers spend almost as many hours engaged in professional learning and debriefing as face-to-face with students; this includes pre-program professional development, daily co-planning and debriefing time, and weekly coaching. This approach is intended to build capacity within the district, and we recommend strategically selecting faculty from multiple school sites and disciplinary areas, staggering staffing so that approximately half of the team is new each year, and identifying opportunities for veteran faculty to assume leadership roles at their home school sites.

Nevertheless, only a small fraction of a district's personnel will have the opportunity to teach within a Language Explorer program; thus, it is important to identify additional ways to support stakeholders in learning with and from newcomer and emergent plurilingual students. Common approaches include districtwide professional development, live or virtual tours of Language Explorer classrooms, presentations by Language Explorer teachers and students, and reports to site and district leadership.

In AUHSD, task force members suggested many strategies for helping the larger community learn about the experiences, aspirations, and assets of its newcomer students, as well as the ways radically inclusive teaching transforms the classroom community. Some of the district's most impactful approaches included:

- creating a program where educators and administrators "shadow" emergent plurilingual students in order to gain a more complete understanding of their daily experiences (see Soto, 2021, for more on shadowing programs);
- inviting student filmmakers from the district's Summer Film Academy to create a mini-documentary about the program;
- hosting "learning walks" where district administrators, school board trustees, and elected officials visit Language Explorer programs, meet newcomer students and their teachers, and reflect on their observations;
- offering hands-on parent information nights, family literacy events, classroom tours, and high-visibility closing ceremonies so that students' families can experience school as a welcoming, plurilingual space in which newcomer students are valued;
- hiring plurilingual students enrolled in other district-based leadership programs as interns and co-teachers within Language Explorer classrooms (see Figure 9.2);
- offering site visits for preservice teachers and administrators, teachers from outside districts, and students at local universities; and
- inviting newcomer and emergent plurilingual students to co-present about the Language Explorer programs during school board meetings.

In addition to functioning as professional learning for district personnel, activities like these provide an invaluable opportunity to establish a programmatic identity for a district's newcomer programming and strategically engage diverse stakeholders as partners and advocates (see Figure 9.2).

Moreover, as newcomer and emergent plurilingual students come to believe that their voices are valued within the district, they gain the confidence to act as leaders. In AUHSD, for example, graduates of the Language Explorer programs have created newcomer welcome videos to help orient incoming students, serve as language ambassadors at their school sites, and assume positions as "peer tutors" (a formal academic appointment that carries weight on college applications). Additional resources related to these efforts, including copies of student-created documentaries and welcome videos, readings on student shadowing, and protocols for learning walks, are available on our companion website.

Figure 9.2. Members of AUHSD's 2019 Language Explorer Advocacy Team

From left to right, Diana Fujimoto (Curriculum Specialist, AUHSD), Renae Bryant (Director of Plurilingual Services, AUHSD), Natalie Tran (Chair, Department of Secondary Education, California State University Fullerton), Ferran Rodríguez-Valls (Professor, Department of Secondary Education, California State University Fullerton), Alison Dover (Associate Professor, Department of Secondary Education, California State University Fullerton), Debbie Pham (Principal, Magnolia High School) and Roxanna Hernandez (Principal, Katella High School).

Maximize Your Impact

One of AUHSD's signature programs is AIME (Anaheim's Innovative Mentoring Experience), a 2020 California School Board Association Golden Bell-recognized program that matches high school students with professional internships, mentoring, and scholarship funding. As part of their effort to position newcomer programming as an essential aspect of the district's identity, they began hiring an AIME intern for each of our Summer Language Academy classes. The following quote illustrates how decisions like this position newcomer program have a far wider impact:

Having the students not only use English, and practice their English, and refine their skills but also use their native language was really new because you would normally think, oh, if you're going to go to school in America, and you're in America, then you should learn English and put that as your priority. But allowing them to connect back to their culture and their native language, I think it's really good and so positive.

As someone who is also not an immigrant, like of first generation, but
   my first language is also Vietnamese, [I know] that clash of "Oh, am I
   Vietnamese? Am I American?" but [there is] that unison that comes
   together in using both of my languages and having that identity of being
   Vietnamese-American. I saw that the project itself really helped them to
   emphasize that.

I [also] didn't expect that it would be more about civic engagement and how
   we can help our community, but when we were diving into that, I loved
   that they all had different perspectives that came from their cultural
   perspectives as well. I could see that the differences that they had, from
   like Ellie who was from Mexico and Haneul who was from Korea, so
   having them converse together and see [how their] views [were] the
   same and different was really nice.

Acting as an intern within a Language Explorer classroom stretched
this student's thinking about her own and her peers' identities as multilingual scholars. This is just one of the ways AUHSD leverages their Language
Explorer programs to build community and promote reflection about the
unique assets each student brings to the district.

*Reflection questions: Who are the student leaders within your district or school
site? How many are newcomer or emergent plurilingual students, and what types
of cultural and linguistic diversity exists among those students? How can you increase opportunities for culturally, linguistically, and academically diverse students
to learn about and from one another?*

These types of programmatic initiatives also serve an important rhetor-
ical function: They position programs for newcomer and emergent plurilingual students as valuable, necessary, and treasured aspects of the district's
identity. This is critically important in establishing programmatic and fiscal
sustainability, and furthers efforts to institutionalize culturally and linguistically sustaining practices systemwide.

PLAN FOR SUSTAINABILITY

As we note throughout this book, braving up requires a comprehensive re-
visioning of what it means to teach and learn in a plurilingual community.
There is no quick fix, and true transformation will take time, resources, and

commitment. Thus, we encourage districts to carefully consider how they will fulfill the promises they make to newcomer and emergent plurilingual students, especially in times of political, fiscal, or administrative change.

One of the ways districts can ensure sustainability is to build programmatic identity and tell the story of their programs. In AUHSD, for example, district leaders are strategic about their approach to institutionalizing their work with and on behalf of newcomer and emergent plurilingual students. Many members of their Newcomer Task Force have become involved in other districtwide initiatives (such as those related to technology, content area programming, parental engagement, International Baccalaureate programs, and Career and Technical Education); this ensures the experiences of newcomer students are both visible and considered systemwide. District leaders engage the media and community organizations as partners in developing and disseminating narratives about their newcomer programs (see the sidebar "Tell Your Story") and have presented about their Language Explorer programs at the county, state, and national level. AUHSD has received numerous high-visibility awards (including the 2018 Orange County Department of Education Cultural and Linguistic Responsiveness Award and the 2019 California School Boards Association Golden Bell Award) for their Language Explorer programs, and hosts hundreds of visiting educators, administrators, and elected officials. Collectively, these efforts raise the prominence and profile of AUHSD's Language Explorers programs and help situate them as part of the district's core identity, which helps ensure programmatic stability from year to year.

Tell Your Story

With the increase of communication through social media, it is important that school districts are purposeful about how they "brand" themselves (Sheninger & Rubin, 2017); when a district doesn't choose to tell its own story, it runs the risk that their story may be told for them. In AUHSD, communication about their Language Explorer programs is as carefully planned as other aspects of the program: leaders take pictures and post them on social media, write "Friday Updates" to the school board, plan site tours and invite honorees months in advance, and involve the media whenever possible.

Media outlets are always looking for a "feel-good" story, and AUHSD's Language Explorer programs provide an opportunity to highlight the strengths of newcomer students and communities. AUHSD includes media releases as part of their program orientation, ensuring that they have active or passive releases for all participating students. Program leaders work with the superintendent's office and the district's public information officer to invite the media for special events, family nights, program tours, and closing ceremonies. When creating press releases for events, AUHSD includes quotes from students and leaders, as well as pictures; many media outlets use these as the backbone for their stories. The district also engages community partners as potential media connections, which has helped to generate stories in linguistically diverse local and international outlets.

Questions: What is the story you want to tell about your district's newcomer and emergent plurilingual students? What systems, processes, and protocols around engaging the media already exist in your organization? What are some innovative ways you can tell the story? Is there a way to engage your scholars and other stakeholders in telling your story?

It is important to strategically position newcomer programs as part of a district's overarching academic mission, calendar, and funding structure. For example, in addition to helping districts meet local, state, and federal goals related to multiliteracy, programs like the Language Explorers function as academic enrichment classes in which newcomer students have the opportunity to explore and leverage their full linguistic repertoires. They are not remedial programs to meet perceived gaps in students' academic or linguistic foundation. This framing is both intentional and strategic; within many districts, "enrichment" is typically interpreted as primarily for academically elite and linguistically dominant students. However, by positioning the Language Explorers as an enrichment program—one in which students earn elective credit; go on field trips; access smaller class sizes and mentorship; engage in creative, project-based learning; develop leadership skills; and present to outside audiences—leaders can situate newcomer programming to serve the broader educational mission of the district. Thus, in addition to state and federal funds earmarked for "English Learners" (such as Title III), for example, we encourage districts to consider how to embed Language Explorer programs within their annual calendar, budget, accountability metrics, grant applications, staffing and recruitment plans, and other district-wide initiatives related to curriculum development and professional learning.

Moreover, when a school district labels programs with adjectives such as "remedial" or "enrichment," it is clearly establishing a *stance* on how they are approaching, perceiving, and including the linguistic richness of emergent plurilingual students. If the school district *designs* a program under the umbrella of enrichment, it is a testimony to the value it places on who newcomer and emergent students are and what they bring to the community. In contrast, when a school district builds a remedial program, it is demonstrating that it sees its students as having deficits that need correction. Thus, in a process that mirrors the translanguaging *corriente* (current) (García, Ibarra Johnson, & Seltzer, 2017), braving up requires districts to interrogate their stance, design intentionally, and *shift* from "enriching language learners" to allowing themselves to *be enriched by* the students' linguistic repertoires. Radically inclusive teaching emerges when local educational agencies invite, affirm, amplify, and transform as they listen to students' voices.

IF YOU WERE TO CHANGE THE WORLD: NEXT STEPS IN RADICALLY INCLUSIVE TEACHING

In closing, we refer back to the question Paola posed to her students: What would you do if you were to change the world? What are your first steps in re-visioning what schooling can be? Throughout this book, we have presented Language Explorers as a model to inspire you to brave up your pedagogies and methodologies. We have invited you to learn with us, listen to our students, and discover alongside our teachers. We have asked you to reflect on your practices and positionality, and to take your own first steps toward re-visioning what schooling could be.

Whenever we wrap up a workshop, we are reminded that attending a professional learning session is easy; every teacher leaves the room with ideas to implement in their classroom. Here, however, we urge you to do something bigger: to pose larger questions, to take and demand decisive action. Will you continue using "Band-Aid teaching" in an attempt to lessen the bleeding that language learners experience on a daily basis? Or will you eliminate the curricular, pedagogical, and institutional tools that slice, subjugate, and razor the edges of students' humanity? We cannot solve the problem by simply covering up the wounds we ourselves create. Instead, we have to brave up and ask ourselves the types of critical questions we pose to our own students: Who am I? Why do I do what I do? In which behaviors will I engage? How will I amplify the skills that I have? And most importantly, what is next? Where do I start?

We are walking beside you all through this process. We must; we need to keep telling one another, "You have to be brave." In doing so, we will keep remembering to be accountable to ourselves and our students, and to make others accountable as well. Radical teaching does not happen in isolation; changing systems of oppression is a collective process. Ubuntu: I am brave because we are brave.

Notes

1. In this manuscript, we have chosen to capitalize the word "White" when referring to racialized identity groups and systems (e.g., White people, White gaze, Whiteness). This was not a decision made lightly, and there is significant controversy within the field about whether—and when—to capitalize this word. Our own thinking on this question continues to evolve. Some critical race scholars (e.g., Crenshaw, 1988; Gotanda, 1991) argue that capitalizing "White" risks reinforcing White supremacy, while others argue that choosing not to capitalize White "contribute[s] to its seeming neutrality and thereby grant[s] [Whiteness] the power to maintain its invisibility" (Ewing, 2020). In deciding how to approach this question within this book, we grappled with the racial context of teaching and teacher education: In the United States, education is a field that has been dominated by White people and, at the time of publication, 79 percent of teachers in the United States identify as White (NCES, 2021). Thus, the sociolinguistic ideologies and educational practices that we critique throughout this book have largely been created and perpetuated by White people and educators, and reflect the impact and interests of Whiteness. Moreover, we anticipate that readers of this book are likely to reflect the racial demographics of the field overall. Ultimately, therefore, we choose to capitalize White in an effort to challenge White people's ability to "maintain the fiction that race is other people's problem, that they are mere observers in a centuries-long stage play in which they have, in fact, been the producers, directors, and central actors" (Ewing, 2020). In so doing, we seek not to reinforce racial dominance, but rather to disrupt the race evasion that is endemic within teaching and teacher education (see Kohli, Dover, Jayakumar, Lee, Henning, Comeaux, Nevárez; Hipolito, Carreno Cortez, & Vizcarra,, 2021). We hope this decision provokes conversation and invite readers to interrogate how their own racial identities and raciolinguistic lenses shape their languaging within and beyond the classroom. Would you have made the decision we did? Why or why not? See Chapters 2 and 3 for additional discussion of raciolinguistics, Whiteness, and the impact of the White gaze on languaging practices.

2. Proposition 58 was passed in 2016, and reversed almost 20 years of English-only immersion requirements associated with California's Proposition 227. With the passage of Proposition 58, districts were required to solicit parent

and community input when designing multilingual and English Learner programs, required to offer bilingual education for English Learners, and authorized to expand dual immersion programs for native and non-native English speakers.

3. Teachers we refer to by first name only are pseudonyms.

4. Portions of Chapter 3 have been previously published in Dover, A. G. & Rodríguez-Valls, F. (2018). Learning to "brave up": Collaboration, agency, and authority in multicultural, multilingual, and radically inclusive classrooms. *International Journal of Multicultural Education, 20*(3), 59–79. Reprinted with permission of IJME.

5. Micrography is an artistic technique where text is used to create high-contrast line drawings of people, places, or symbols. See Chapter 4 for examples.

6. All students referenced by first name alone are pseudonyms.

7. We intentionally avoid the use of the adjective "academic language," as it perpetuates a linguistic hierarchy that positions English as the primary and exclusive language of scholars. Instead, we use phrases like "disciplinary vocabulary" or "subject area English" to emphasize that students are stretching their linguistic repertoire by incorporating new terms and resources, not replacing their current way of languaging with something "better."

8. In English: I think of soccer, tacos [and] Mexico because it's my dear country that I am never going to forget.

9. In English: "I thought this summer would be boring but it was the best summer of my life. I met many people who now occupy a very special place in my heart, between [my three teachers] they are the best teachers and I wish I could have you in my school."

10. In English: "Removing all the toxic people from my life."

11. In English: "They are like the sisters that I could never have and I thank you because from the day they both came into my life they put a great light that no one could turn off, [and] put a very big smile on my face."

12. In English: "This photo is when I left school. That moment I will never forget it because I spent many happy moments with my friends and teachers. I was very sad and happy because I would know more schools, but I would miss my friends and teachers. On that day my friends and I started dancing until the dance was over. All my friends were wearing dresses and I saw that many children of eighth grade started to cry and I was going to cry because some of my friends were going to other schools, some were going to Mexico with their parents."

13. In English: "When I was little I had hard time understanding. . . . English was hard for me but with all the things I learned and they have taught me it is not as hard as I thought . . . how they present things in a friendly way how they teach you to lose your fears to speak English . . . I like to learn new things about the language . . . And I like the sense of humor to learn things . . . like

the tree that has surface, shallow and deep culture . . . learn about different languages and cultures and we can achieve what was hard to learn."

14. The concept of linguistic fragility is an adaptation of Robin DiAngelo's (2018) construct of White fragility, referring to the defensive reactions White people enact when their beliefs, position, and privileges are questioned. In similar terms, linguistic fragility represents the fearful or defensive reactions enacted by members of linguistically dominant groups. For additional analysis of linguistic dominance and fragility, see Dover and Rodríguez-Valls (2018).

References

Agarwal, R., Epstein, S., Oppenheim, R., Oyler, C., & Sonu, D. (2010). From ideal to practice and back again: Beginning teachers teaching for social justice. *Journal of Teacher Education, 61*(3), 237–247.

Alim, H. S., & Paris, D. (2017). What is culturally sustaining pedagogy and why does it matter? In D. Paris & H. S. Alim (Eds.), *Culturally sustaining pedagogies: Teaching and learning for justice in a changing world* (pp. 1–21). Teachers College Press.

Annamma, S.A., Boelé, A. L., Moore, B. A., & Klingner, J. (2013). Challenging the ideology of normal in schools. *International Journal of Inclusive Education, 17*(12), 1278–1294.

Anzaldúa, G. (1987). *Borderlands/la frontera: The new mestiza*. Aunt Lute Books.

Arao, B., & Clemens, K. (2013). From safe spaces to brave spaces. In L. Landreman (Ed.), *The art of effective facilitation* (pp. 135–150). ACPA Press.

Aronson, B., & Laughter, J. (2016). The theory and practice of culturally relevant education. *Review of Educational Research, 86*(1), 163–206.

Archambault, L., Shelton, C., & McArthur, L. (2021). Teachers beware and vet with care: Online educational marketplaces. *Phi Delta Kappan, 102*(8), 40–44.

Artiga, S., Corallo, B., & Pham, O. (2020). Racial disparities in COVID-19: Key findings from available data and analysis. Kaiser Family Foundation. https://www.kff.org/racial-equity-and-health-policy/issue-brief/racial-disparities-covid-19-key-findings-available-data-analysis/

Au, W. (2013). What's a nice test like you doing in a place like this? The edTPA and corporate education "reform." *Rethinking Schools, 27*(4), 22–27.

Bajaj, M., & Suresh, S. (2018). The "warm embrace" of a newcomer school for immigrant & refugee youth. *Theory into Practice, 57*(2), 91–98.

Baldaquí Escandell, J. M. (2009). La inseguretat lingüística i l'aprenentatge de les llengües minoritzades: Reflexions des del País Valencià. *Revista Catalana de Pedagogia, 6*(177–197).

Bartolomé, L. (1994). Beyond the methods fetish: Toward a humanizing pedagogy. *Harvard Educational Review, 64*, 173–195.

Basaran, H. (2017). Egen bearbetning för att visualisera språksystem inom translanguaging. https://frokenhulya.wordpress.com/

Bell, D. (1980). *Brown v. Board of Education* and the interest–convergence dilemma. *Harvard Law Review, 93*(3), 518–533.

Bernstein, K. (2020). *(Re)defining success in language learning: Positioning, participation, and young emergent bilinguals at school.* Multilingual Matters.

Besecker, M., & Thomas, A. (2020). *Student engagement online during school facilities closures: An analysis of LA Unified secondary students' schoology activity from March 16 to May 22, 2020.* Independent Analysis Unit, LAUSD.

Bonilla-Silva, E. (2006). *Racism without racists: Color-blind racism and the persistence of racial inequality in the United States.* Rowman & Littlefield Publishers.

Boostrom, R. (1998). "Safe spaces": Reflections on an educational metaphor. *Journal of Curriculum Studies, 30*(4), 397–408.

Borrero, N., & Sanchez, G. (2017). Enacting culturally relevant pedagogy: Asset mapping in urban classrooms. *Teaching Education, 28*(3), 279–295.

Bronfenbrenner, U. (1977). Toward an experimental ecology of human development. *American Psychologist, 32*(7), 513–531.

Browne, M. L., Acevedo, A., & Gatwood, O. (2020). *Woke: A young poet's call to justice.* Roaring Brook Press.

Buehl, D. (2014). *Classroom strategies for interactive learning* (4th ed.). International Reading Association.

Bulté, B., & Housen, A. (2012). Defining and operationalising L2 complexity. In A. Housen, F. Kuiken, & I. Vedder (Eds.), *Dimensions of L2 performance and proficiency: Complexity, accuracy, and fluency in SLA* (pp. 21–46). John Benjamins.

Bussert–Webb, K. M., Masso, H. M., & Lewis, K. A. (2018). Latinx children's push and pull of Spanish literacy and translanguaging. *The Qualitative Report, 23*(11), 2648–2669.

Cacho, L. M. (2012). *Social death: Racialized rightlessness and the criminalization of the unprotected.* New York University Press.

California Alliance of Researchers for Equity in Education. (2020). The shift to online education during and beyond the COVID-19 pandemic: Concerns and recommendations for California. http://www.care-ed.org

California Department of Education [CDE]. (2015). English language arts/English language development framework for California public schools: Kindergarten through grade 12 https://www.cde.ca.gov/ci/rl/cf/elaeldfrmwrksbeadopted.asp

California Department of Education [CDE]. (2021a). Facts about English Learners in California. https://www.cde.ca.gov/ds/ad/cefelfacts.asp

California Department of Education [CDE]. (2021b). State Seal of Biliteracy. https://www.cde.ca.gov/sp/el/er/sealofbiliteracy.asp

Caranfa, A. (2006). Voices of silence in pedagogy: Art, writing and self-encounter. *Journal of Philosophy of Education, 40*(1), 85–103.

Chandra, S., Chang, A., Day, L., Fazlullah, A., Liu, J., McBride, L., Mudalige, T., & Weiss, D. (2020). *Closing the K–12 digital divide in the age of distance learning.* Common Sense Media.

Chen, D. (2020). Visual languaging: Exploring visualisation in language and cognitive development through a pluriliteracies model in online EFL classrooms. Unpublished doctoral dissertation. University of Edinburgh. http://dx.doi.org/10.13140/RG.2.2.27149.77289

Choi, Y. (2003). *The name jar*. Dragonfly Books.

Choi, Y. (2013). Teaching social studies for newcomer English language learners: Toward culturally responsive pedagogy. *Multicultural Perspectives, 15*(1), 12–18.

Cisneros, S. (1994). *Hairs/pelitos*. Knopf.

Colato Laínez, R., & Lacámara, L. (2016). *Mamá the alien: Mama la extraterrestre*. Lee & Low Books.

Commonwealth of Massachusetts. (2002). An act relative to the teaching of English in public schools. https://malegislature.gov/Laws/SessionLaws/Acts/2002/Chapter386

Costa, K. (2020). Poll: California parents very concerned about children falling behind during school closures. The Education Trust–West. https://west.edtrust.org/press-release/poll-ca-p

Council of Europe. (2007). From linguistic diversity to plurilingual education: Guide for the development of language education policies in Europe. Language Policy Division. https://rm.coe.int/16802fc1c4

Creese, A., & Blackledge, A. (2010). Translanguaging in the bilingual classroom. *Modern Language Journal, 94*(1), 103–115.

Crenshaw, K. W. (1988). Race, reform, and retrenchment: Transformation and legitimation in antidiscrimination law. *Harvard Law Review, 101*(7), 1331–1387.

Crenshaw, K. (1989). Demarginalizing the intersection of race and sex: A Black feminist critique of antidiscrimination doctrine, feminist theory and antiracist politics. *University of Chicago Legal Forum, 1989*(1), 139–167.

Cummins, J. (1979). Linguistic interdependence and the educational development of bilingual children. *Review of Educational Research, 49*, 222–251.

Davis, C. (2018). Writing the self: Slam poetry, youth identity, and critical poetic inquiry. *Art/Research International: A Transdisciplinary Journal, 3*(1), 114–131.

De Jong, E. J., & Howard, E. (2009). Integration in two-way immersion education: Equalising linguistic benefits for all students. *International Journal of Bilingual Education and Bilingualism, 12*(1), 81–99.

de los Ríos, C. V., Seltzer, K., & Molina, A. "Juntos somos fuertes": Writing participatory corridos of solidarity through a critical translingual approach. *Applied Linguistics, 2021*, 1–14.

Delgado, M. (2015). *Urban youth and photovoice: Visual ethnography in action*. Oxford University Press.

Delpit, L. (2006). *Other people's children: Cultural conflict in the classroom*. New Press.

Delpit, L. (2009). Language diversity and learning. In A. Darder, M. P. Baltodano, & R. D. Torres (Eds.), *The critical pedagogy reader* (pp. 324–337). Routledge.

Desmond Tutu Peace Foundation. (2017). Mission and philosophy. http://www
.tutufoundationusa.org/desmond-tutu-peace-foundation/

DiAngelo, R. (2018). *White fragility: Why it's so hard for white people to talk about racism.* Beacon Press.

Dover, A. G. (2009). Teaching for social justice and K–12 student outcomes: A conceptual framework and research review. *Equity & Excellence in Education, 42*(4), 506–524.

Dover, A. G. (2013). Teaching for social justice: From conceptual frameworks to classroom practices. *Multicultural Perspectives, 15*(1), 3–11.

Dover, A. G. (2015). "Promoting acceptance" or "preparing warrior scholars": Variance in teaching for social justice vision and praxis. *Equity & Excellence in Education, 48*(3), 361–372.

Dover, A. G. (2016). Teaching for social justice and the Common Core: Justice-oriented curriculum for language arts and literacy. *Journal of Adolescent & Adult Literacy, 59*(6), 517–527.

Dover, A. G. (2018). Your compliance will not protect you: Agency and accountability in urban teacher preparation. *Urban Education.* https://doi.org/10.1177/0042085918795020

Dover, A. G., Henning, N., & Agarwal-Rangnath, R. (2016). Reclaiming agency: Justice-oriented social studies teachers respond to changing curricular standards. *Teaching and Teacher Education, 59,* 457–467.

Dover, A. G., & Rodríguez-Valls, F. (2018). Learning to "brave up": Collaboration, agency, and authority in multicultural, multilingual, and radically inclusive classrooms. *International Journal of Multicultural Education, 20*(3), 59–79.

Dover, A. G., & Schultz, B. (2018). Turning towards students: Adopting a student-centered stance in mandate-centered times. In G. Holl, D. Gollnick, & L. Quinn (Eds.), *The handbook of teaching and learning* (pp. 199–223). Wiley.

Ek, L. D., Sánchez, P., & Quijada Cerecer, P. D. (2013). Linguistic violence, insecurity, and work: Language ideologies of Latina/o bilingual teacher candidates in Texas. *International Multilingual Research Journal, 7,* 197–219.

Ellis, R. & Barkhuizen, G. (2005). *Analysing learner language.* Oxford University Press.

Espada, M. (1990). *Rebellion is the circle of a lover's hands.* Curbstone Press.

Esquivel, P. (2021, April 4). In California, a million English learners are at risk of intractable education loss. *Los Angeles Times.* https://www.latimes.com/california/story/2021-04-04/how-covid-distance-learning-hurt-california-english-learners

Esquivel, P., & Blume, H. (2020, July 16). L.A. Latino, Black students suffered deep disparities in online learning, records show. *Los Angeles Times.* https://www.latimes.com/california/story/2020-07-16/latino-and-black-students-hard-hit-with-disparities-in-their-struggle-with-online-learning

Estrada, P. (2014). English learner curricular streams in four middle schools: Triage in the trenches. *Urban Review, 46*(5), 535–573.

Ewing, E. L. (2020, July 1). I'm a black scholar who studies race. Here's why I capitalize "White." *Zora.* https://zora.medium.com/im-a-black-scholar-who -studies-race-here-s-why-i-capitalize-white-f94883aa2dd3

Fisher, D., & Frey, N. (2013). *Better learning through structured teaching: A frame work for the gradual release of responsibility* (2nd ed.). Association for Supervision and Curriculum Development [ASCD].

Flores, N., & García, O. (2013). Translanguaging across the bilingual continuum. In D. Little, C. Leung, & P. Van Avermaet (Eds.), *Managing diversity in education: Languages, policies, pedagogies* (pp. 243–246). Multilingual Matters.

Flores, N., & Rosa, J. (2015). Undoing appropriateness: Raciolinguistic ideologies and language diversity in education. *Harvard Review Press, 85*(2), 149–171.

Flores, N., & Rosa, J. (2019). Bringing race into second language acquisition. *Modern Language Journal, 103*(51), 145–151.

Flores, N. & Schissel, J. L. (2014). Dynamic bilingualism as the norm: Envisioning a heteroglossic approach to standard-based reform. *TESOL Quarterly, 48*(1), 454–479.

Fraise, N., & Brooks, J. (2015). Toward a theory of culturally relevant leadership for school–community culture. *International Journal of Multicultural Education, 17*(1), 6–21.

Fránquiz, M. E., & Salinas, C. S. (2011). Newcomers to the U.S.: Developing historical thinking among Latino immigrant students in a central Texas high school. *Bilingual Research Journal, 34*(1), 58–75.

Freire, J. A., & Valdez, V. E. (2017). Dual language teachers' stated barriers to implementation of culturally relevant pedagogy. *Bilingual Research Journal, 40*(1), 55–59.

Freire, P. (1970/2000). *Pedagogy of the oppressed.* Bloomsbury Press.

Freire, P. (2005). *Teachers as cultural workers: Letters to those who dare teach.* Westview Press.

Fruja Amthor, R., & Roxas, K. (2016). Multicultural education and newcomer youth: Re–imagining a more inclusive vision for immigrant and refugee students. *Educational Studies, 52*(2), 155–176.

García, O. (2009). Education, multilingualism and translanguaging in the 21st century. In A. Mohanty, M. Panda, R. Phillipson, & T. Skutnabb-Kangas (Eds.), *Multilingual education for social justice: Globalising the local* (pp. 128–145). Orient Blackswan.

García, O., Ibarra Johnson, S., & Seltzer, K. (2017). *The translanguaging classroom: Leveraging student bilingualism for learning.* Caslon.

García, O., Kleifgen, J., & Falchi, L. (2008). From English language learners to emergent bilinguals. *Equity matters: Research review No. 1.* The Campaign for Educational Equity. Teachers College Press. https://files.eric.ed.gov /fulltext/ED524002.pdf

García, O., & Seltzer, K. (2016).The translanguaging current in language education. In B. Kindenberg (Ed.), *Flerspråkighet som resurs* [Multilingualism as a resource] (pp. 19–30). Liber.

García, O., & Torres-Guevara, R. (2009). Monoglossic ideologies and language policies of education of U.S. Latina/os. In E. M. Murillo, S. A. Villenas, R. Trinidad Galván, J. Sánchez Muñoz, C. Martiínez, & M. Machado-Casas (Eds.), *Handbook of Latinos in education: Theory, research and practice* (pp. 182–193). Routledge.

García, O., & Tupas, R. (2018). Doing and undoing bilingualism in education. In A. De Houwer & L. Ortega (Eds.), *Cambridge handbook of bilingualism* (pp. 390–407). Cambridge University Press.

Gay, G. (2000). *Culturally responsive teaching: Theory, research, and practice*. Teachers College Press.

Gee, J. P. (2004). *Situated language and learning: A critique of traditional schooling*. Routledge.

Genesee, F., Lindholm-Leary, K., Saunders, W., & Christian, D. (2005). English language learners in U.S. schools: An overview of research findings. *Journal of Education for Students Placed at Risk, 10*(4), 363–385.

Gotanda, N. (1991). A critique of "Our Constitution Is Color-Blind." *Stanford Law Review, 44*(1), 1–68.

Guttiérez, K. D. (2008). Developing a sociocritical literacy in the third space. *Reading Research Quarterly, 43*(2), 148–164.

Habermas, J. (1987). *The theory of communicative action, Vol. I: Reason and the rationalization of society*. Beacon. (Original work published 1981.)

Hemphill, D., & Blakely, E. (2019). English language learning in globalized third spaces: From monocultural standardization to hybridized translanguaging. In D. Macedo (Ed.). *Decolonizing foreign language education* (pp. 220–240). Routledge.

Henning, N., Dover, A. G., Dotson, E. K., & Agarwal-Rangnath, R. (2018). Storying teacher education policy: Critical counternarratives of curricular, pedagogical, and activist responses to state-mandated teacher performance assessments. *Education Policy & Analysis Archives, 26*(26), 1–33.

Hernandez, S. J. (2017). Are they all language learners? Educational labeling and raciolinguistic identifying in a California Middle School Dual Language Program. *CATESOL Journal, 29*(1), 133–154.

Holquist, S., & Porter, T. (2020, June 3). Culturally responsive leading and learning: Addressing equity through student and family voice. Pacific Regional Equity Laboratory [blog post]. https://ies.ed.gov/ncee/edlabs/regions/pacific/blogs/blog27_culturally-responsive-leading-and-learning_addressing-equity.asp#

Kim, P., & Sánchez, S. (2015). *Here I am*. Curious Fox.

Kiramba, L. K. (2019). Heteroglossic practices in a multilingual science classroom. *International Journal of Bilingual Education and Bilingualism, 22*(4), 445–458.

Kleon, A. (2010). *Newspaper blackout*. HarperPerennial.

Kleyn, T., López, D., & Makar, C. (2015). What about bilingualism? A critical reflection on the edTPA with teachers of emergent bilinguals. *Bilingual Research Journal, 38*(1), 88–106.

Kohl, H. (1995). *"I won't learn from you": And other thoughts on creative maladjustment*. The New Press.

Kohli, R. (2021). *Teachers of color: Resisting racism and reclaiming education*. Harvard Educational Press.

Kohli, R., Dover, A. G., Jayakumar, U., Lee, D., Henning, N., Comeaux, E., Nevárez, A., Hipolito, E., Carreno Cortez, A.,& Vizcarra, M. (2021). Toward a healthy racial climate in teacher education: Systematically centering the well-being of teacher candidates of color. *Journal of Teacher Education, 73*(1), 52–65.

Kohli, R., & Solórzano, D. (2012). Teachers, please learn our names!: Racial microaggressions and the K–12 classroom. *Race Ethnicity and Education, 15*(4), 441–462.

Krashen, S. D. (1985). *The input hypothesis: Issues and implications*. Addison-Wesley Longman.

Krulatz, A., & Iversen, J. (2020). Building inclusive language classroom spaces through multilingual writing practices for newly-arrived students in Norway. *Scandinavian Journal of Educational Research, 64*(3), 372–378.

Kuntz, D., Shrodes, A., & Cornelison, S. (2017). *Lost and found cat: The true story of Kunkush's incredible journey*. Dragonfly Books.

Ladson-Billings, G. (1995). Toward a theory of culturally responsive pedagogy. *American Educational Research Journal, 32*(3), 465–491.

Lee, J. S. (2010). Culturally relevant pedagogy for immigrant children and English language learners. *National Society for the Study of Education, 109*, 453–473.

Lindholm-Leary, K., & Hernández, A. (2011). Achievement and language proficiency of Latino students in dual language programmes: Native English speakers, fluent English/previous ELLs, and current ELLs. *Journal of Multilingual and Multicultural Development, 32*(6), 531–545.

Lindsey, R. B., Nuri-Robins, K. Terrell, R. D., & Lindsey, D. B. (2018). *Cultural proficiency: A manual for school leaders* (4th ed.). Corwin Press.

Lippi-Green, R. (2011). *English with an accent*. Routledge.

Lopez, A. A., Turkan, S., & Guzman-Orth, D. (2017). *Conceptualizing the use of translanguaging in initial content assessments for newly arrived emergent bilingual students* (Research Report No. RR-17-07). Educational Testing Service.

Lopez, F. A. (2016). Culturally responsive pedagogies in Arizona and Latino students' achievement. *Teachers College Record, 118*(5), 1–42.

Lynn, M. (2014, March 19). Making culturally relevant pedagogy relevant to aspiring teachers. *Diverse Issues in Higher Education*. http://diverseeducation.com/article/61280/

Lyon, G. E. (1999). *Where I'm from: Where poems come from.* Absey and Company.

Madeloni, B., & Gorlewski, J. (2013). Wrong answer to the wrong question: Why we need critical teacher education, not standardization. *Rethinking Schools, 27*(4). http://www.rethinkingschools.org/archive/27_04/27_04_madeloni-gorlewski.shtml

Martin-Beltrán, M. (2014). "What do you want to say?" How adolescents use translanguaging to expand learning opportunities. *International Multilingual Research Journal, 8,* 208–230.

Massachusetts Department of Education. (2007). 2006 MCAS results by subgroup by grade and subject. https://profiles.doe.mass.edu/mcas/subgroups2.aspx?linkid=25&orgcode=01370000&fycode=2006&orgtypecode=5&.

Matam, P., Acevedo, E., & Yamazawa, G. (2014). Unforgettable [Video file]. Button Poetry/YouTube. https://youtu.be/Xvah3E1fP20

Matias, C. E., & Mackey, J. (2016). Breakin' down whiteness in antiracist teaching: Introducing critical whiteness pedagogy. *Urban Review, 48*(1), 1–19.

Matsuda, M. (2020, March 3). I'm a superintendent. My students' activism is key to their academic success. *EdWeek.* https://www.edweek.org/leadership/opinion-im-a-superintendent-my-students-activism-is-key-to-their-academic-success/2020/03

McCrea, B. (2021, March 15). AI is changing the workforce. At this district, it's changing curriculum too. *EdSurge.* https://www.edsurge.com/news/2021-03-15-ai-is-changing-the-workforce-at-this-district-it-s-changing-the-curriculum-too

Milner, IV, H. R. (2020). *Start where you are, but don't stay there: Understanding diversity, opportunity gaps and teaching in today's classrooms* (2nd ed.). Harvard Education Press.

Mitchell, C. (2016, February 24). California leader puts spotlights on long-term English learners. *EdWeek.* https://www.edweek.org/leaders/2016/california-leader-puts-spotlights-on-long-term-english-learners

Mitchell, K. (2012). English is not all that matters in the education of secondary multilingual learners and their teachers. *International Journal of Multicultural Education, 14*(1), 1–21.

Moll, L. C., Amanti, C., Neff, D., & Gonzalez, N. (1992). Funds of knowledge for teaching: Using a qualitative approach to connect homes and classrooms. *Theory into Practice, 31*(2), 132–141.

Morrison, T. (n.d.). Toni Morrison on writing without the "white gaze." [Video]. PBS. https://www.pbs.org/wnet/americanmasters/toni-morrison-on-writing-without-the-white-gaze/14874/

Morrison, T. (2001, May 4). A conversation between Toni Morrison and Frank Mc-Court. [Video]. YouTube. https://www.youtube.com/watch?v=oP_-m7V58_I

National Center for Education Statistics. (2021). *Characteristics of public school teachers.* https://nces.ed.gov/programs/coe/indicator/clr

Negri, A. & Hardt, M. (2005). *Multitude: War and democracy in the age of empire.* Penguin Press.

New York University Metropolitan Center for Research on Equity and the Transformation of Schools. (n.d.). Guidance on culturally responsive-sustaining remote education: Centering equity, access, and educational justice. https://crehub.org/s/NYU-Metro-Center-Guidance-on-Culturally-Responsive-Sustaining-Remote-Teaching-and-Learning-2020-1-1.pdf

Nieto, S. (2013). *Finding joy in teaching students of diverse backgrounds: Culturally responsive and socially just practices in U.S. schools*. Heinemann.

Oyserman, D., Harrison, K., & Bybee, D. (2001). Can racial identity be promotive of academic efficacy? *International Journal of Behavioral Development, 25*(4), 379–385.

Papay, J. P., Murnane, R. J., & Willett, J. B. (2010). The consequences of high school exit examinations for low-performing urban students: Evidence from Massachusetts. *Educational Evaluation and Policy Analysis, 32*, 5–23.

Paris, D. (2012). Culturally sustaining pedagogy: A needed change in stance, terminology, and practice. *Educational Researcher, 41*(3), 93–97.

Paris, D., & Alim, S. (Eds.) (2017). *Culturally sustaining pedagogies: Teaching and learning for justice in a changing world*. Teachers College Press.

Parr, T. (2009). *It's okay to be different*. Little, Brown and Company.

Pearson, P. D., & Gallagher, M. C. (1983). The instruction of reading comprehension. *Contemporary Educational Psychology, 8*(3), 317–344.

Pennycook, A. (2019). From translanguaging to translingual activism. In D. Macedo (Ed.), *Decolonizing foreign language education* (pp. 169–195). Routledge.

Picower, B. (2011). Resisting compliance: Learning to teach for social justice in a neoliberal context. *Teachers College Record, 113*(5), 1105–1134.

Picower, B. (2021). *Reading, writing and racism: Disrupting racism in teacher education*. Beacon Press.

Quezada, R., Rodríguez-Valls, F., & Lindsey, R. (2016). *Teaching and supporting migrant children of farm worker families: A cultural proficiency approach*. Rowman & Littlefield.

Rodriguez, G. (2020). From troublemakers to pobrecitos: Honoring the complexities of survivorship of Latino youth in a suburban high school. *Journal of Latinos and Education*, 1–18. https://doi.org/10.1080/15348431.2020.1796672

Rodríguez, S., Monreal, T., & Howard, J. (2020): "It's about hearing and understanding their stories": Teacher empathy and socio-political awareness toward newcomer undocumented students in the New Latino South. *Journal of Latinos and Education, 19*(2), 181–198.

Rodríguez-Izquierdo, R. M. (2015). Estudio de las actitudes hacia la escuela y de las expectativas educativas de los estudiantes de origen inmigrante. *Education Policy Analysis Archives, 23*(127). https://doi.org/10.14507/epaa.v23.2161

Rodríguez-Valls, F. (2009). Culturally relevant poetry: Creating Esperanza (hope) with stanzas. *Multicultural Education, 17*(1), 10–13.

Rodríguez-Valls, F. (2016). Pedagogy of the immigrant: A journey towards inclusive classrooms. *Teachers and Curriculum, 16*(1), 41–48.

Rosa, J. (2018). *Looking like a language, sounding like a race: Raciolinguistic ideologies and the learning of Latinidad.* Oxford University Press.

Roxas, K., & Gabriel, M. L. (2016). Amplifying their voices. *Educational Leadership, 73*(5), 78–81.

Roxas, K. C., Gabriel, M. L., & Becker, K. (2017). "Mexicans are like thieves and bad people, and we're not really like that": Immigrant youth use photovoice to counter racism and discrimination. *Journal of School Counseling, 15*(19), n19.

Salazar, M. (2013). A humanizing pedagogy: Reinventing the principles and practice of education as a journey toward liberation. *Review of Research in Education, 37,* 121–148.

Salinas, C., Sullivan, C., & Wacker, T. (2007). Curriculum considerations for late-arrival high school immigrant students. *Journal of Border Educational Research, 6*(2), 55–67.

Seltzer, K. (2020). '"My English is its own rule'": Voicing a translingual sensibility through poetry. *Journal of Language, Identity and Education 19*(5), 297–311.

Shapiro, S. (2014). "Words that you said got bigger": English Language Learners' lived experiences of deficit discourse. *Research in the Teaching of English, 48*(1), 386–406.

Sheninger, E., & Rubin, T. (2017). *BrandED: Tell your story, build relationships, and empower learning.* Jossey-Bass.

Shin, N. (2017). The effects of the initial English Language Learner classification on students' later academic outcomes. *Educational Evaluation and Policy Archives, 40*(2), 175–195.

Sintos Coloma, R. (2020) Decolonizing urban education. *Educational Studies, 56*(1), 1–17.

Skehan, P. (2003). Task-based instruction. *Language Teaching, 35*(1), 1–14.

Sleeter, C. (2001). Preparing teachers for culturally diverse schools: Research and the overwhelming presence of whiteness. *Journal of Teacher Education, 52*(2), 94–106.

Sleeter, C. E. (2011). *The academic and social value of ethnic studies: A research review.* National Education Association.

Solórzano, D. G., & Ornelas, A. (2002). A critical race analysis of advanced placement classes: A case of educational inequality. *Journal of Latinos and Education, 1*(4), 215–229.

Solsona-Puig, J., Capdevila-Gutiérrez, M., & Rodríguez-Valls, F. (2018). La inclusividad lingüística en la educación multilingüe de California: Coexistencia de las variedades y registros de lengua para enriquecer el aula de inmersión dual. *Educación y Educadores, 21*(2), 219–236.

Sonu, D., & Aguilar, L. P. (2017). When poetry visits you: Liberating the human spirit in second graders. *Social Studies and the Young Learner, 30*(2), 24–29.

Soto, G., & Jenkins, H. (2009). *Oranges: Ode to family photographs*. Rubicon.

Soto, I. (2021). *Shadowing multilingual learners* (2nd ed.). Corwin.

Suárez-Orozco, C., Pimentel, A., & Martin, M. (2009). The significance of relationships: Academic engagement and achievement among newcomer immigrant youth. *Teachers College Record, 111*(3), 712–749.

Suárez-Orozco, C., Suárez-Orozco, M., & Todorova, I. (2008). *Learning a new land: Immigrant students in American society*. Belknap Press of Harvard University Press.

Tafolla, C. (1992). In memory of Richi. In *Sonnets and Salsa* (pp. 66–67). Wings Press.

Tarone, E., & Swain, M. (1995). A sociolinguistic perspective on second language use in immersion classrooms. *Modern Language Journal, 79*(2), 166–178.

Telgemeier, R. (2016). *Ghosts*. Graphix.

Thompson, K. D., Umansky, I. M., & Porter, L. (2020). Examining contexts of reception for newcomer students. *Leadership and Policy in Schools, 19*(1), 10–35.

Tochon, F. V. (2019). Decolonizing world language education: Toward multilingualism. In D. Macedo (Ed.), *Decolonizing foreign language education* (pp. 264–281). Routledge.

Tuck, E., & Gorlewski, J. (2016). Racist ordering, settler colonialism, and edTPA: A participatory policy analysis. *Educational Policy, 30*(1), 197–217.

Tuckman, B. W. (1965). Development sequence in small groups. *Psychological Bulletin, 63*(6), 384–399.

United States Census Bureau. (1990). General population characteristics: New York, section 1 of 2. https://www2.census.gov/library/publications /decennial/1990/cp-1/cp-1-34-1.pdf

United States Department of Education. (2015). Our nation's English learners: What are their characteristics? https://www2.ed.gov/datastory/el -characteristics/index.html

United States Department of Education. (2019). Supporting English learners through technology: What districts and teachers say about digital learning resources for English Learners Volume I: Final report. https://www2.ed .gov/rschstat/eval/title-iii/180414.pdf

United States Department of Education. (2021). Public school enrollment (updated May 2021). Institute of Education Science: National Center for Education Statistics. https://nces.ed.gov/programs/coe/indicator/cga

Valdés, G. (2015). Latin@s and the intergenerational continuity of Spanish: The challenges of curricularizing language. *International Multilingual Research Journal, 9*(4), 253–273.

Valenzuela, A. (1999). *Subtractive schooling: U.S.–Mexican youth and the politics of caring*. State University of New York Press.

Valenzuela, A. (2016). *Growing critically conscious teachers: A social justice curriculum for educators of Latino/a youth*. Teachers College Press.

Viorst, J. (1984). *If I were to change the world and other worries: Poems for children and their parents*. Atheneum Books for Young Readers.

Vogel, S., & García, O. (2017). Translanguaging. In G. Noblit & L. Moll (Eds.), *Oxford research encyclopedia of education*. Oxford University Press. 10.1093/ac refore/9780190264093.013.181

Vygotsky, L. V. (1930/1962). *Thought and language*. Boston, MA: The MIT Press.

Wei, L. (2011). Moment analysis and translanguaging space: Discursive construction of identities by multilingual Chinese youth in Britain. *Journal of Pragmatics*, *43*, 1222–1235.

Wei, L. (2018). Translanguaging as a practical theory of language. *Applied Linguistics*, *39*(1), 9–30.

Wilhelm, J. D., Baker, T. N., & Dube, J. (2001). *Strategic reading: Guiding students to lifelong literacy, 6–12*. Boynton/Cook.

Williams, C. P. (2020). *School closure and English learners: A review of COVID-19 operations written reports*. Californians Together. https://californianstogether.app .box.com/s/bktwfcbv8kj4bqqjn3gdflpcumau18um

Williams, K. L., Mohammed, K., & Stock, C. (2009). *My name is Sangoel*. Eerdmans Books for Young Readers.

Wolf-Quintero, K., Inagaki, S., & Kim, H.-Y. (1998). *Second language development in writing: Measures of fluency, accuracy, & complexity*. University of Hawai'i, Second Language Teaching & Curriculum Center.

Wubs-Mrozewicz, J. (2020). The concept of language of trust and trustworthiness: (Why) history matters. *Journal of Trust Research*, *10*(1), 91–107.

Yang, G. L. (2006). *American born Chinese*. First Second Books.

Yeon Kim, H., & Suárez-Orozco, C. (2015). The language of learning: The academic engagement of newcomer immigrant youth. *Journal of Research on Adolescence*, *25*(2), 229–245.

Zenkov, K., & Harmon, J. (2009). Picturing a writing process: Photovoice and teaching writing to urban youth. *Journal of Adolescent and Adult Literacy*, *52*(7), 575–584.

Index

Note: Names followed by (teacher) or (student) are pseudonyms.

About the Authors

Alison G. Dover is an associate professor in the Department of Secondary Education at California State University, Fullerton. She holds a doctorate in social justice education from the University of Massachusetts, Amherst, and has taught English Language Arts and service learning in diverse urban school districts in Massachusetts and Rhode Island. Dr. Dover works extensively with local and national students, educators, and school communities to advance social justice, agency, and culturally sustaining pedagogies in K–12 and teacher education. She is co-author of *Preparing to Teach Social Studies for Social Justice: Becoming a Renegade* (2016, Teachers College Press) and has written numerous journal articles and book chapters related to literacy, equity-oriented approaches to teacher education, and teaching for social justice. Dr. Dover holds leadership roles in the American Educational Research Association (Division K: Teaching and Teacher Education) and the California Alliance of Researchers for Equity in Education (CARE-ED), and is the principal investigator for a Spencer Foundation Research-Practice Partnership Grant titled Project LEARN: Language, Equity and Action Research with Newcomer Students.

Fernando (Ferran) Rodríguez-Valls is a professor at California State University, Fullerton (CSUF). Dr. Rodríguez-Valls has created partnerships with school districts and local educational agencies to develop and implement community-based [bi/multi]literacy programs. At CSUF, Dr. Rodríguez-Valls coordinates the Bilingual Authorization Program and the World Languages Program. In this capacity, he recruits and prepares future educators to design, implement, and evaluate asset-based and heteroglossic practices. Dr. Rodríguez-Valls's publications, including his first book, *Teaching and Supporting Migrant Children of Farm Worker Families: A Cultural Proficiency Approach* (Rowman & Littlefield, 2016), focus on equitable and linguistically inclusive methodologies for emergent plurilingual, newcomer, and [im]migrant students as well as on the sociocultural factors affecting their academic achievement, educational continuity, and school engagement. Dr. Rodríguez-Valls has directed and co-directs grant projects in which teacher candidates have the opportunity to create brave learning spaces where teaching overpowers instruction, where learning surpasses drilling, where languages conquer monolingualism, and where critical thinking eradicates fanaticism and a fake sense of monoglossic and univocal identity.

Renae Bryant serves as the director of Plurilingual Services at Anaheim Union High School District (AUHSD) in Anaheim, California, where she leads efforts to increase student access, opportunity, equity, and success through the Plurilingual/English Learner, World Languages, and 2019 CSBA Golden Bell Award–winning Spanish and Vietnamese Dual Language Immersion programs. Previously at Westminster School District, Dr. Bryant led a team to implement the first Vietnamese Dual Language Immersion program in California, which was awarded the California School Board Associations Golden Bell in 2017. She is the founder and facilitator of the Leadership Book Chat (#Ldrshpbkchat), where she leads national book studies about equity and leadership in education. Dr. Bryant serves as the director of Public Relations for the Association of California School Administrators Region 17 and as president of the California Association for Bilingual Education Riverside Chapter #6, and she was recently named a 2020 Woman of Distinction for California's 34th Senate District by Senator Thomas J. Umberg. Dr. Bryant earned a doctorate in organizational leadership at the University of La Verne in 2017 and completed the ACSA Superintendents Academy, AASA/USC Urban Superintendents Academy, and the AASA Aspiring Female Superintendents Academy, and she is currently enrolled in the Stanford EdLEADers Program. Dr. Bryant has served as an award-winning National Board Certified elementary and secondary teacher, as well as a site and district administrator.